The Evolutionary Universe
and
Self-Conscious Human Being

Others books by the Author

- Phenomenal Consciousness and Mind-Body Problem in East-West Persspective; 2019; ISBN: 978-81-246-0946-0
- Saṁsāra and Nirvāṇa: A Unifying Vision; 2017; ISBN: 978-81-246-0894-4
- Science of Consciousness: A Synthesis of Vedānta and Buddhist Philosophy; 2023; ISBN: 978-81-246-1204-0
- Thinker, Thought and Knowledge in East-West Perspective; 2021; ISBN: 978-81-246-1044-2

The Evolutionary Universe and Self-Conscious Human Being

— East-West Perspective —

V.N. Misra

DK PRINTWORLD
Publishers of Indian Traditions

Cataloging in Publication Data — DK

[Courtesy: D.K. Agencies (P) Ltd. <docinfo@dkagencies.com>]

Misra, V.N., author.

The evolutionary universe and self-conscious human being : East-West perspective / V.N. Misra.

pages cm

Includes bibliographical references.

ISBN 9788124612811 (HB)

1. Cosmology. 2. Self-consciousness (Awareness) 3. Hindu philosophy. 4. Space and time. 5. Causation. 6. Philosophy and science. 7. Physics – Philosophy. I. Title.

LCC BD511.M57 2024 | DDC 113 23

ISBN: 978-81-246-1281-1

First published in India in 2024

Printed and published by:

D.K. Printworld (P) Ltd.

Regd. Office: "Vedaśrī", F-395, Sudarshan Park

(Metro Station: ESI Hospital), New Delhi – 110015

Phones: (011) 4172 2626, 98713 94815

e-mail: indology@dkprintworld.com

Website: www.dkprintworld.com

Preface

In this study two things are involved: the evolutionary universe (*brahmāṇḍa*) and self-conscious human being (*piṇḍa*). The former is "*out* there" and the latter is "out here". If latter does not exist, it is indeed difficult to know or perceive "out there". This is mainly because "out here" has the mind through which "out there" is known. Whether "out there" has mind or not, it is indeed, difficult to know. For "out there", it is a scientifically accepted back that the sun is "out there" 93 million miles away from earth.

Space is perceived by outer sense and time in the form of inner sense. Both (space and time) cannot exist in themselves but that exist in us (human beings have representations of space–time). This is viewed by conscious human being subjectivity as time and the former is perceived objecting as space.

i. The Sāṁkhya–Yoga philosophy is embodied the concept of *sattva*, *rajas* and *tamas*. These three are in a sense comparable to the proton, the electron and the neutron. The proton provides the coalescence or the form of the atom. The electron gives us energy and proton provides the access (Catalina 1968: 32-33).

ii. The atoms of Vaiśeṣika philosophy are not the atoms of modern chemistry, nor can we think as homogeneous ethereal or electronic particles.

iii. All the things are happening within the time and space. It can be recognized through events.

My gratitude is beyond words to Shri M.L. Pandit for encouraging me to write book in philosophy.

I express my gratitude to the authors from whose books the passages have been quoted in different chapters of this book.

I am, indeed, grateful to Shri Susheel K. Mittal, Director, D.K. Printworld, for his sincere efforts in publication of the book.

Buddha Pūrṇimā **V.N. Misra**
23 May 2024
New Delhi

Contents

Introduction

THIS study specifically attempts:

i. In the evolutionary universe and self-conscious being, the former is "out" there and like the latter is "out" here. If the latter "out" here does not exist, it is indeed difficult to know "out" there. This is mainly because human being is self-conscious, and therefore, he knows himself as well as the evolutionary universe.

ii. The Sāṁkhya-Yoga philosophy is embodied with the concepts of *sattva*, *rajas* and *tamas*. These three are in a sense comparable to the proton, the electron and the neutron. The proton provides the coalescence or the form of the atom. The electron gives us energy and proton provides the mass (Catalina 1968: 32-33).

iii. The atoms of Vaiśeṣika philosophy are not the atoms of modern chemistry, nor can we think as homogeneous ethereal or electronic particles.

iv. All the things are happening within the time and space. It can be recognized through events.

The universe of Big Bang itself had zero size and was infinitely hot. But as it expanded, the temperature of the radiation decreased. One second after Big Bang the temperature had fallen about 10,000 million degrees.

> This is about 1,000 times the temperature at the centre of the sun, but temperatures as high as this are reached in H-bomb explosions.
> – Hawking 1988: 120

At this time:

> The universe would have contained mainly protons, electrons and neutrons (extremely light particles that are affected only by the weak force and gravity) and their anti-particles, together with some protons and neutrons. – Hawking 1988: 120

On the basis of the above observation, an inference may be drawn that the universe at Big Bang seems to have taken place because of the existence of particles (electrons, photons and neutrons) in seed form before Big Bang. This shows that the origin of the universe is based on something rather than nothing. This may be supported by the Greek view that creation out of nothing is impossible (Glattfeldor 2018: 535).

The observations regarding particles are, however, quite intriguing. In the case of electrons, it is stated that something like mind is already present in the electron (ibid.: 534). This works as a particle as well as a wave. Further, electron is negative particle forming constituent of an atom. The electron moves in orbits round a central atomic nucles (Narlikar 1978: 253). Yet, it is indeed difficult to say the particle like electron has mind. This is mere imagination. Similar is the case with photon. It is stated that photon has a degree of consciousness. In this context, the following observation regarding photon is worth stating:

> The idea is not that photons are intelligent or thinking [...]. But the thought is, maybe, photons might have some elements of subjective feeling, some primitive precusor to consciousness.
> – Glattfeldor 2018: 531

The photon is a particle associated with light. According to quantum theory, light consists of packet of energy (Narlikar 1978: 256). If one thinks that particles like electron and proton have mind and subjective feeling, it may be said that these statements are mere conjunctors.

The earth came into existence about 4.6 billion years ago along with the sun (i.e. solar system came into existence). We are treating *saṁsāra* with the beginning of human beings because it became known mainly when human being came into existence. The evolution of human being, started quite late: it has a history of about 6 million years (Capra and Luisi 2014: 242 (see fig. 11.1)). This indicates that the earth existed for about more than 4 billion years in potential form to generate the conditions for the evolution of human life.

However,

> the world, the universe, the cosmos and the earth were synonymous terms in the geocentric concept. Such an idea has now been discarded. It has been realized that the Earth occupies an insignificant dot in the illimitable universe. – Panda 2008: 163

Yet, scientists have compared the earth (*saṁsāra*) having life with the universe. This is evident from the observation:

> The very structure of the universe is explainable only through biocentrism. The universe is fine-tuned for life, which makes perfect sense as life creates the universe, not the other way round. The universe is simply the complete spatio-temporal logic of the self.
> – Lanza and Berman 2009: 93

In the above statement, "life creates universe, not the other way round" does not seem to be appropriate for life came from material universe itself. The universe has taken long time for about 4 billion years after solar system coming into existence to create conditions for the evolution of human life on this earth. This may be supported by the following observation as given in the same book:

> Everything started 13.7 billion years ago when the entire universe materialized out of nothingness. Explaining ever since, first rapidly, then more slowly, the expansion started speeding up once again some 7 billion years ago due to an unknown repulsive force, which is the main constituent of the cosmos. All structures and events are created entirely randomly, given the four fundamental forces and a host of parameters and constants such as the universal pull of gravity. Life began 3.9 billion years

> ago on Earth and possibly elsewhere at unknown times. It too occurred by the random collisions of molecules, which in turn are made of combinations of one or more of the ninety-two natural elements. Consciousness or awareness arose of life in a manner that remains mysterious. – Lanza and Berman 2009: 155

In the context of evolution of human life on Earth, the following recent observation deserves attention:

> To chart the unfolding of life on Earth, we have to use a geological time scale, on which periods are measured in billions of years. It begins with the formation of the planet Earth, a fire ball of molten lava, around 4.5 billion years ago. We can distinguish three broad ages in the evolution of life on Earth, each extending for 1-2 billion years, and each containing several distinct stages of evolution. The first is the prebiotic age, in which the conditions for the emergence of life and the first protocells were formed. It lasted 1 billion years, from the formation of the earth to the creation of the first cells, the beginning of life, around 3.5 billion years ago. The second age, extending for a full 2 billion years, is the age of the microcosm, in which bacteria and other micro-organisms invented the basic processes of life and established the global feedback loops for the self-regulation of the Gai system. – Capra and Luisi 2014: 240

It is, further, observed:

> The Earth was cold enough to host the first mild organic reactions around 3.9 billion years ago and the first fossils are 3.45 billion years old. – Ibid. 220 (see fig. 10.2)

But how transition has taken place from non-life to life? We do not have as yet any answer to this question. It has, however, been accepted:

> This development was triggered by rapid brain growth at the dawn of human evolution, about 4 million years ago, when language, reflective consciousness, the ability to make and use tools, and organized social relations all evolved together. ... The size of the brain has been an important determinant for human

> development, since brain size is widely believed to be proportional to intelligence. – Capra and Luisi 2014: 249-50

In this context, it may be stated that intelligent beings can exist only in the expanding phase of the universe (Hawking 1988: 152). Since the universe is still expanding, indicating thereby that the growth of intelligent beings is almost certain. This in way assures better future for human beings in expanding phase of the universe, provided of course the scientific developments are used for the peaceful coexistence of human beings.

Origin and Duration of the Universe (Based on Indian Philosophy)

It is observed that

> if we calculate the lifespan of our own world (an aeon or a day of Brahmā) in terms of human years it comes to 4,320 million years. – Upadhyaya 1983: 388

This is calculated as follows:

> 1 day and night of gods = 1 year of human beings.
>
> 1 year or 360 days and nights of gods = 360 years of human beings.
>
> 1 *yuga* or 12,000 years of gods = 1200 × 360 = 4,320,000 years of human beings.
>
> 1,000 *yugas* of gods or 1 day of Brahmā or 1 aeon of human beings = 4,320,000 × 1000 = 4,320,000,000 years of human beings. – Ibid.

It may be noted that the above estimate of 4.3 billion years of lifespan of our world is more or less similar to 4.6 billion years of solar system, including the sun and the earth (Panda 2008: 198). In corresponding to the age of our world (i.e. 4.3 billion years) there is no estimate available regarding the human evolution in Indian philosophy. Such an estimate is, however, available in the theosophical literature. It is stated that the first dawn of human life had taken place about 18,000,000 years ago (Barborka 1998: 304). It may be noted:

> The "dawn of human life" refers to the awakenment of the mind-principle during the third race and not to man's first appearance on the Fourth Round. – Upadhyaya 1983: 305

According to theosophy, there are seven root races.

It may be stated that theosophical thinkers have admitted that the various assumptions for estimating the years for evolving human life may not be acceptable to the followers of science (ibid.: 117). Yet, we are comparing the first dawn of human life that had taken place about 18,000,000 years ago, as mentioned above. Against this, the scientific estimate works out only 6 million years (see Capra and Luisi 2014: 242). That apart, the fact remains that even if we compare the theosophicals' estimate of 18 million years of human life with that of lifespan of our world of 4.3 billion years, the gap between the two works out to be about 4 billion years. In another study also it is observed:

> While there may be some disputes on the exact date, it appears reasonable to assume that around 0.75 to 1 billion years after the birth of the solar system including the earth, the first primitive life forms such as bacteria appeared on earth. – Menon 2004: 261

If one takes the upper estimate of 1 billion years for evolving human life, the gap between the evolution of human life and existence of solar system, which came into existence around 4.3 billion years, works out to be more than 3 billion years. Now the question is: why *Brahman*, being the creator, sustainer and dissolver of the entire universe (for details see Swami Gambhirananda 2000: 14), has taken more than 3 billion years (after coming the solar system into existence) to create conditions for evolving human life. It is, indeed, beyond the human comprehension to understand such a big gap between the age of solar system and human evolution. Under such a situation, one has to draw an inference like the one which has already been drawn:

> *Perhaps philosophy is from beginning to end a cobweb of necessary imagination* (emphasized by italics). – Moitra 1988: 4

That apart, the other fact is that the universe is still expanding. So is the case of human intelligence. Therefore, it is all the more difficult to justify *Brahman* as the creator of the universe. The first cause of the universe is, indeed, insoluable. It would be reasonable to see the role of the creator in the creation itself. This is evident from *Chāndogya Upaniṣad* III.14.1 which begins with the Sanskrit word सर्वं खल्विदं ब्रह्म (*sarvaṁ khalvidaṁ brahma*) meaning, everything here is verily *Brahman*. The creation itself is treated as creator. This may be supported by another fact that the causes of the events are seen mainly in effects according to Indian philosophy of Sāṁkhya and Vedānta. So it would be reasonable to look at the creator through the creation itself.

The Universe and Its Saṁsāra (Empirical World)

SCIENTIFIC VIEWS ON THE ORIGIN OF THE UNIVERSE

According to scientific cosmology, the universe came into existence in the Big Bang about 14 billion years ago. "Our particular galaxy, the Milky Way is about 10 billion years old" (Larson 2003: 176). However, our sun, being a second generation star, was formed about 4.6 billion years. The earth came along with the sun. The life began 3.9 billion years ago on earth as mentioned earlier. It means that the entire universe was lying as dark energy for about 10 billion years. Human formation became quite late in the universe and that too only on earth, which occupies an insignificant dot in the universe.

The universe at the Big Bang itself had zero-size and was infinitely hot. But as it expanded, the temperature of the radiation decreased. One second after the Big Bang the temperature had fallen to about ten thousand million degrees.

> This is about 1,000 times the temperature at the centre of the sun, but temperatures as high as this are reached in H-bomb explosions. At this time the universe would have contained mainly photons, electrons and neutrons (extremely light particles that are affected only by the weak force and gravity) and their anti-particles, together with some protons and neutrons.
>
> – Hawking 1988: 117

This is further explained as follows:

> Our own sun contains about 2 per cent of these heavier elements because it is a second or third generation star, formed some 5,000 million years ago out of a cloud of rotating gas containing the debris of earlier supernovas. Most of the gas in that cloud went to form the sun or got blown away, but a small amount of the heavier elements collected together to form the bodies that now orbit the sun as planets like earth. – Ibid.: 120

The earth at the beginning was very hot and without an atmosphere. The early atmosphere was such that no one could have survived because there was no oxygen (ibid.). However, the process of evolution

> that led to the development more and more complicated, self-reproducing organisms. The first primitive forms of life consumed various materials including hydrogen sulfide and released oxygen. This gradually changed the atmosphere to the composition that it has today and allowed the development of higher forms of life such as fish, reptiles, mammals and ultimately the human race. – Ibid.: 121

However, the smooth regions of galaxies and stars are those where the conditions were right for "the development of complicated self-replicating organisms like ourselves who were capable of asking the question: Why is the universe so smooth?" This is an example of the application of what is known as the anthropic principle, which can be paraphrased as, "We see the universe the way it is because we exist" (ibid.: 124).

The notion of entropy is popularly described as the measure of disorder in a system (Bohm and Peat 1987: 137). This has, however, been used here to describe the odds against those that permit the emergence of life. The anthropic principle has two versions: the weak and the strong. Hawking has justified the weak anthropic principle, which is stated as follows:

> One example of the use of the weak anthropic principle is to "explain", why the Big Bang occurred about 10,000 million years ago – it takes about that long for intelligent beings to evolve. As explained above, an early generation of stars first had to form. These stars converted some of the original hydrogen and helium into elements like carbon and oxygen, out of which we are made. The stars then exploded as supernovas, and their debris went to form other stars and planets, among them those of our solar system, which is about 5,000 million years old. The first 1,000 or 2,000 million years of the earth's existence were too hot for the development of anything complicated. The remaining 3,000 million years or so have been taken up by the slow process of biological evolution, which has led from the simplest organisms to beings, who are capable of measuring time back to the Big Bang (Hawking 1988: 124).

Now the question is "why is the universe the way we see it?" The answer is then simple: "If it had been different, we would have not be here" (ibid.: 125).

However, the most interesting aspect of scientists' view is that "the universe is self aware through us" (Goswami 1995: 190). If the universe became self-aware through us, it means that the universe in itself is not self-aware. In this context, it may be stated that whatever is in the cosmos (*brahmāṇḍa*) is also in *piṇḍa*, meaning thereby that whatever is in the universe, the same thing exists in human beings, but it may not be the other way round. This is mainly because human being came into existence very late in the universe as mentioned earlier. Therefore, we have learned a lot from the universe, the universe in itself cannot learn much from human being despite the fact that human beings have influenced to some extent the functioning of the universe; particular instance is the recent climate change. Yet, one wonders whether the universe in itself became aware through us, but we are certainly aware of the universe; for the obvious reason that our lives depend upon the universe to a great extent.

VEDĀNTIC VIEWS ON THE ORIGIN OF THE UNIVERSE AND ITS STATUS

While commenting on *Brahmasūtra* 1.1.2, it is stated:

> That omniscient and omnipotent source must be *Brahman* from which occur the birth, continuance and dissolution of this universe that is manifested through name and form, that is associated with diverse agents and experiences, that provides the support for actions and results, having well-regulated space, time, and causation, and that defies all thoughts about the real nature of its creation. – Swami Gambhirananda 2000: 14

Let us see how *Brahman* is defined in Advaita Vedānta.

According to Vedānta, *Brahman* is uncaused, it does not undergo any change. Further, it is neither dependent on nor be contradicted by anything. *Brahman* is self-existent and it is beyond time, space and causality. In fact, *Brahman* is eternal, infinite, absolute existence. However, *Brahman* is Existence (*sat*), Consciousness (*cit*) and Bliss (*ānanda*).

This view is now supported by a scientist also. It is observed that

> anything that we do not observe directly exists only as potential or more mathematically speaking as a haze of probability. "Nothing", said Wheeler, exists, until it is observed.
>
> – Lanza and Berman 2009: 181

However, according to Sri Ramana Maharshi, Dr̥ṣṭi-sr̥ṣṭivāda means that

> the world comes into existence simultaneously with the appearance of the "I"-thought and that it ceases to exist when the "I"-thought is absent. This theory is known as *dr̥ṣṭi-sr̥ṣṭi,* or simultaneous creation, and it says, in effect, that the world which appears to an *ajñānī* is a product of the mind that perceives it, and that in the absence of that mind it ceases to exist.
>
> – Godman 1992: 175

Dṛṣṭi-Sṛṣṭivāda

According to this theory,

> the world is an objective reality governed by laws of cause and effect, which can be traced back to a single act of creation. It includes virtually all Western ideas on the subject from the Big Bang theory to the biblical account in Genesis. – Godman 1992: 176

Buddhist's View of the Universe and Empirical World (Saṁsāra)

UNIVERSE

According to Buddhists, all substances in the universe are referred to a matter (*rūpa*). The principal elements are:

> (1) abstract earth (*paṭhavi*), (2) abstract water (*āpo*), (3) abstract air (*vāyo*), and (4) abstract heat (*tejo*). – Ranasinghe 1957: 43

However, each of these great abstract elements (*mahābhūtas*) has two chief characteristics. These are stated below:

i. abstract earth: to harden and to soften,
ii. abstract water: to flow and to paste,
iii. abstract air: to expand and to contract, and
iv. abstract heat: to heat and to cool (ibid.: 44).

It is further stated that

> no substance is formed in the universe without the mixing of all four principal elements, the presence of each element affecting the features in each substance in the eight different manners.
> – Ibid.

Each unit of abstract element of any substance

> penetrates into all others, and all others penetrate into each other. It is such union of units of abstract elements that settles into forming substances. – Ranasinghe 1957: 45

Constitution of Atom

The atom (*rūpa-kalāpa*) is the last possible particle of a substance. Its formation is stated below:

> In an atom, one of the four great abstract elements is reduced to unity, whilst the units of the other three abstract elements may be present in larger numbers. We may, therefore, get an atom consisting of a total of, say, 1,111 units of all abstract elements divided in a proportion such as; abstract earth 1,000 units, abstract heat 100 units, abstract water 10 units and abstract air 1 unit.
>
> – Ramasinghe 1957: 47

It is further stated:

> The explanation of the Buddha in regard to the manner in which the atoms are formed has to be thoroughly comprehended by us, because this knowledge is indispensable in comprehending the manner in which man takes conception at birth, grows up, and finally dies. This knowledge also helps us to understand the manner in which this Earth and the Universe came into being, how they grew up, and how they dissolve in the end and form yet another universe over again. – Ibid.: 49

The most important aspect of atom according to the Sautrāntika Buddhists is that

> the atoms being substantially or ultimately real (*dravya-sat* or *parmārtha-sat*) can cause the corresponding consciousness. But Diṅnāga argued, the atoms being formless themselves cannot contribute the form or image to the corresponding cognitive state. Thus, the atoms do not satisfy the second condition being the objective support of consciousness. – Matilal 1997: 236

Now let us see how electron, proton and neutron are treated in the dualistic philosophy of Sāṁkhya–Yoga.

Prakr̥ti

The *prakr̥ti* is treated as the natural principle, which happens to be the causal background of the whole objective world. It is derived from the Sāṁkhya theory of causation (Satkāryavāda). According to this theory, the effect is originally existent in material cause prior to its manifestation as an effect (Catalina 1968: 25).

> The cause evolves into the effect and, yet as cause, remains what it is. As effect it is modified that is the effect is the cause modified. All which exists is a transformation of one substance, their cause. Causation is transformation: cause and effect being different positions of the same thing in the time sequence, the antecedent position being the cause and the consequent position the effect. – Woodroffe 2001: 208

The Sāṁkhya theory of causation has been summed up very well in a statement that "the effect and the cause are explicit and implicit states of the same substance" (quoted in Catalina 1968: 26). This may be explained by the example of cloth which is actually not different from the thread from which it is woven. It is, thus, evident that the effect exists in the material cause prior to its production in the phenomenal world. An inference from this theory has, however, been drawn that the *prakṛti* happens to be ultimately the cause of the world of objects (ibid.: 27).

The *prakṛti* as source of matter and mind has three *guṇas*: *sattva*, *rajas* and *tamas* (Woodroffe 2001: 208). However, two observations about the *guṇas* may be worth noting, viz.:

1. This tripartite process (*guṇas*) may be described either with objectivity or with reference to subjectivity because it underlies both sorts of description (Larson 2003: 184; 2009), and
2. although *prakṛti* being quite subtle cannot be perceived directly, yet it may be accepted on inferential grounds as science has done with the atom (Catalina 1968: 29). This is explained below:

> This concept is embodied in the modern scientific conception of the construction of the atom. In this scientific conception, the atom has the proton, the electron and

> the neutron. These three are, in a sense, comparable to the concept of the Sāṁkhya of the *sattva*, *rajas* and *tamas* respectively. The proton provides the coalescence or the form of the atom, the electron gives us energy, and the proton provides the mass. – Catalina 1968: 32-33

The *prakṛti* happens to be the principle of unconsciousness and works in association with consciousness. It may reveal consciousness or obscure consciousness.

> When it is said that *sattva* reveals consciousness, what it meant is that it does so relative to the operation of *tamas*. Consciousness is self-revealing. – Woodroffe 2001: 208

However, when *prakṛti* suppresses the revealing factor (*sattva*), "it obscures consciousness and is called *tamas*. But both these actions involve activity and this is the *rajas guṇa*" (ibid.). It thus follows that these factors, being the factors of matter and mind, are composing the whole universe. These three *guṇas* affect things differently. For instance, *tamas* affects more gross inorganic matter, whereas *sattva guṇa* reveals consciousness in human beings more predominantly as compared to *rajas* and *tamas*. It may, however, be stated that the *guṇas* – *sattva*, *rajas* and *tamas* – never exist separately from one another (ibid.). The *sattva* and *rajas* predominate in thought, and *tamas* and *rajas* do so in the gross matter (Catalina 1968: 34). In a nutshell, *sattva* is the intelligence stuff of potential consciousness, whereas, *rajas* is the energy stuff, while *tamas* is the mass stuff (ibid.: 32).

It has been further stated:

> All properties can be reduced to their simplest elements: wave motion (*prakāśa*), action (*kriyā*) and position (*sthiti*) at least as far as physical universe is concerned and since these are also the ideas associated with the nature of these *guṇas*. Science has to a certain extent corroborated the theory of *guṇa*.
> – Taimni 1999: 175

The triplicity referred above – *prakāśa-kriyā-sthiti* – is based on the aphorism II.18 of the *Yogasūtra*. It is one of the most important *sūtras* and defines the functional and structural (i.e. subjective and objective) aspects of mental phenomena. The aphorism II.18 of *Yogasūtra* is stated as follows:

> *prakāśa-kriyā-sthiti-śīlambhūtendriyātmakaṁ bhogāpa-vargārthaṁ dṛśyam* ।

This has been translated into English as:

> The seen (objective side of manifestation), consists of the elements (*bhūtas*) and sense organs (*indriyas*), is of the nature of radiation, activity and stability (*sattva*, *rajas* and *tamas*) and has for its purpose (providing the *puruṣa* with) experience and liberation.
> – Taimni 1987a: 364

The subjective aspect is indicated in the phrase *bhūtendriyātmakaṁ*, meaning thereby the mental phenomenon which is

> the interaction between *indriyas* (five sense organs) and the *bhūtas* (the five stimulating agents of sensation). As a result of this interaction on the physical plane, relation between the perceiver and the perceived is established and mental perception in the lowest form of sensation takes place. – Ibid.: 365

The objective (i.e. structural) aspect is hinted at in the word *prakāśa-kriyā-sthiti-śīlam*, meaning thereby that

> the three *guṇas* which are in their essential nature merely different combinations of vibration, activity and stability, which lie at the basis of *bhūtas* and *indriyas*. – Ibid.: 365

Before discussing the above *sūtra*, it may be mentioned that occultism does not deny the physical world consisting of atoms and molecules, and the vibrations playing between them.

> It only interprets in mental terms what orthodox scientist insists on interpreting in material terms even though matter as in usual sense does not exist. – Ibid.: 366

In fact, the essential nature of matter is mainly motion alone. The earlier scientific concept of matter, which was tangle and had a mass and corpuscular at its base, has now been modified. The recent discoveries in physics and chemistry show that matter is essentially radiation (Taimni 1987a: 186).

The Sanskrit words *prakāśa*, *kriyā* and *sthiti* are:

> equivalents of light or radiation (vibration in the subtlest form), motion (i.e. irregular motion as opposed to vibration which is harmonic motion about a mean position) and stability (i.e. absence of motion), respectively. – Ibid.: 367

However, these three words refer to three kinds of motion:

i. harmonic motion (motion of electrons in elliptical orbits in the atom can also be considered as harmonic from a wider perspective) as in the case of light and sound vibrations (ibid.),

ii. simple irregular motion as in the case of particles of a gas or larger objects made of aggregates of atoms and molecules and which are capable of doing work in the scientific sense (ibid.: 367-68), and

iii. stability or absence of relative motion as in the case of molecular structures or larger solid bodies which are aggregates of atoms and molecules (ibid.: 368).

The whole physical world is the play of these three types of motion, which enter into atoms and molecules but also determine their behaviour and properties (ibid.). In this context, it is stated that radiation, according to modern physics, is the ultimate basis of matter (ibid.). It is thus concluded:

> The properties of all substances are determined solely by their inner structures and these inner structures are determined by the combinations of three fundamental types of motion and nothing else. – Ibid.: 368

This shows that matter in the scientific world has now been completely de-materialized.

Prakāśa, *kriyā* and *sthiti* constitute the objective series and the corresponding properties are perceived by the mind as effects of its stimulation constitute the subjective series (Taimni 1987a: 369). Similarly, the *guṇas* too have subjective and objective aspects. The subjective aspect is the nature of the mental images appearing in the mind as the result of simulation of the mind by external objects, whereas the objective aspect is the constitutional basis of properties in different forms and combinations of notions and constitution of particles (ibid.: 370).

The *guṇas* apply in almost every phase of life in Hindu religion and philosophy. In general,

> *sattva* is related to harmony, freedom, bliss, perception; *rajas* to activity, passion and energy and *tamas* to inertia, passivity, will and stability.
> – Ibid.

The objects of self-consciousness is embodied in human beings according to the Vedānta school of Indian philosophy. However, self-consciousness and self-conscious being are one and the same thing. This is explained below.

Transcendental Unity of Self-consciousness

The transcendental unity of self-consciousness has been introduced by Kant, in the second edition of *The Critique of Pure Reason*, which is evident from the following observation:

> As a self-consciousness that is devoid of material content, Kant describes this original unity as "pure" and original apperception (B132); as the condition of the possibility of empirical self-consciousness he also calls it transcendental apperception (A107) in the first edition, and in the second edition the transcendental unity of self-consciousness (B132) or more simply transcendental self-consciousness. The empirical subject which accompanies different representations, judging now this object and now that is in itself diverse. This subject lacks unity in its constant change. It only acquires the identity of the subject through a pre-empirical contribution that does not change, through that

> combining of representations in one consciousness whereby "I represent to myself the identity of the consciousness throughout these representations" (B133). This representation is a synthetic unity of self-consciousness insofar as it accomplishes such a combination, it is an original unity of self-consciousness.
>
> – Hoffe 2010: 156

In the above observation, the transcendental unity of self-consciousness has been mixed up with the notions of subjective and objective. This is explained below:

> The empirical self-consciousness or what he calls empirical apperception or inner sense is subjective, but the transcendent unity of self-consciousness, which is also the synthetic unity of self-consciousness is called objective. It is called objective because of its transcendental role, intersubjective, sameness in all, and also in the sense of being responsible for the concept of object. We can note how the notions of "subjective" and "objective" are being mixed up in Kant. – Chatterjea et al. 2014: 185

The subjective and objective notions of transcendental unity of self-consciousness have been reconciled by Kant. Hoffe (2010: 167) says:

> Kant concludes part proof II and draws the relevant conclusion (Section 26): "the categories are conditions of the possibility of experience, and are therefore valid a priori for all objects of experience" (B 161). The categories are thus capable of "prescribing, as it were, the law to nature" (B 159). Given the thoroughgoing correlation between subjectivity and objectivity, we cannot explain the transcendental structures of subjectivity without simultaneously grasping the pre-empirical features of objectivity. Nor, for the same reason, can we understand the "deduction" without simultaneously considering the lawfulness of nature that is implicit in the categories, the pre-empirical presuppositions of the actual empirical laws of nature. It is only to be expected, therefore, that Kant returns to the question of the synthetic unity of apperception whom he finally completes the "deduction" in the chapter on "The System of All Principles of Pure Understanding". The transcendental "I think" is at once

> the unity of self-consciousness and the unity of nature, and thus both subjectivity and objectivity in one.

It is, however, stated that, "unity of consciousness and unity of object are one and the same thing" (Chatterjea et al. 2014: 162). This has been shown by example as follows:

> If in counting, I forget that the units, which now hover before me, have been added to one another in succession. I should never know that a total is being produced through this successive addition of unit, to unit, and so would remain ignorant of the number. For the concept of number is nothing but the consciousness of this unity of synthesis (ibid.). This is the Kantian move. A number is generated by synthesis a priori synthesis, while counting we are not merely going from one to another, but we are adding the succeeding one to the preceding one. There are three things here. Unity = concept of unity = consciousness of synthesis. – Ibid.

In the above unity three things are not different but they are one. It is known as the transcendental unity of self-consciousness. This unity is treated by Searle (2004: 95) as a unified structure of consciousness which comes to us.

VEDĀNTIC INTERPRETATION OF TRANSCENDENTAL UNITY OF SELF-CONSCIOUSNESS

Consciousness at transcendental level becomes an ontological or metaphysical principle as the Ultimate Reality (Swami Bhajananda 2009: 92). It is further stated:

> Knowledge of transcendental consciousness enables one to face the mystery of death. The survival of consciousness after death is the greatest challenge to science and the greatest support to religion. – Ibid.: 99

However, the transcendental unity of self-consciousness seems to be like *Ātman* (Absolute Reality) of Indian philosophy. It is known, "as *astitva-jñāna* of *Brahman*, i.e. the awareness that *Brahman* exists. It does not need any proof: It is self evident" (Swami Bhajananda 2009: 93). When pure consciousness (Absolute Reality) descends in human being, it becomes self-consciousness, which is referred to as witness self (*sākṣī*). It illumines the mental states: knowledge, ignorance, pain, etc. "The mental states are immediately cognized because of their presence to the witness self" (Swami Satprakashananda 2001a: 91).

Self-consciousness in Hegel's Philosophy

The transition from consciousness to self-consciousness is quite crucial for Hegel. This is mainly because, with self-consciousness we have entered into the native realm of truth.

> The key concern of self-consciousness is with knowledge of the self that is mediated through the object, that is, a self-knowledge that comes through relationships with other objects (practical relationships) and other people (social relationships).
>
> – Williamson 1984: 104

This approach, according to Sartre, avoids solipism (1984: 321). This will be discussed later. However, the inclusion of the other has been justified by Hegel by the fact that in consciousness, the in-itself of the object and the being of the object for another become one and the same thing (Hegel 1998: 104). This in a way protects Hegel's idealism.

In the reflection of self-consciousness the perception of sensible world is involved. In this situation there is no involvement of other beings. This is explained:

> As self-consciousness, it is movement but since what it distinguishes from itself is *only itself as* itself, the difference, as anotherness is *immediately superseded* for it; the difference is *not*, and it (self-consciousness) is only the motionless tautology of: I am I; but since for it the difference does not have the form of *being*, it is not self-consciousness. Hence, otherness is for it in the form of a *being*; or as a *distinct moment*; but there is also for consciousness the unity of itself with this difference as a *second distinct moment*. With that first moment; self-consciousness is in the form of *consciousness;* and the whole expanse of the

> sensuous world is preserved for it, but at the same time only as connected with the second moment; the unity of self-consciousness with itself; and hence the sensuous world is for it an enduring existence. ... The unity of self-consciousness with itself; this unity must become essential to self-consciousness, i.e. self-consciousness is desire in general. Consciousness as self-consciousness, henceforth has a double object; one is the immediate object; that of sense certainty and perception which however *for self-consciousness* has the character of a *negative*; and the second, viz. *itself*, which is the true essence; and is present in the first instance only as opposed to the first object. In this sphere, self-consciousness exhibits itself as the movement in which this anthesis is removed and the identity of itself with itself becomes explicit for it.
>
> – Hegel 1998: 105

However, the notion of self-consciousness gets completed in three moments. These are stated below (ibid.: 110):

i. The pure undifferentiated "I" is its first immediate object.

ii. This immediacy is itself an absolute mediation, it is only as a supersession of the independent object, in other words, it is desire. The satisfaction of desire is, it is true, the reflection of self-consciousness into itself, or the certainty that has become truth.

iii. But the truth of this certainty is really a double reflection, the duplication of self-consciousness. Consciousness has for its object one which, of its own self, posits its otherness or difference as a nothingness, and in so doing is independent. The differentiated, merely *living*, shape does indeed also superstate its independence in the process of life, but it ceases with its distinctive difference to be what it is. The object of self-consciousness, however, is equally independent in this negativity of itself; and thus it is *for itself* a genius, a universal fluid element in the peculiarity of its own separate being; it is a living self-consciousness.

A self-consciousness exists for a self-consciousness. This is mainly because the unity of itself becomes explicit in its otherness. In this context it is observed that the I (ego) happens to be the object of desire, which is independent of the universal indestructible substance, the fluent self-identical essence (Hegel 1998: 110). This is, further, explained below:

> A self-consciousness, in being an object, is just as much "I" as object. With this, we already have before us the notion of *spirit*. What still lies ahead for consciousness is the experience of what spirit is – This absolute substance, which is the unity of the different independent self-consciousnesses which, in their opposition, enjoy perfect freedom and independence; "I" that is "We" and "We" That is "I". It is in self-consciousness, in the notion of *spirit*, that consciousness first finds its turning point, where it leaves behind it the colourful show of the sensuous here-and-now and the night-like void of the supersensible beyond, and steps out into the spiritual daylight of the present. – Ibid.: 110-11

Lordship and Bondage

Self-consciousness lives outside of itself in an other self-consciousness in which it at once looses and also finds itself. However,

> each consciousness then acts itself as much as, it acts on the other, and what it does is as much done by the other to it, as by it to the other consciousness. – Ibid.: 520

Each uses the other as the means by which it achieves self-consciousness. It is, further, observed:

> Self-consciousness must be willing to sacrifice everything concrete for its own infinite self-respect and the similar respect of all others. A life and death struggle therefore ensures between the rival self-consciousness. – Ibid.: 521

> The self-consciousness of the Lord is essentially related to the being of the mere things he uses and uses up, and these he enjoys through the bondsman's self-consciousness. The bondsman prepares and arranges things for the enjoyment of the Lord.

> The self-consciousness of the Lord is likewise essentially related to the self-consciousness of the bondsman through the various punitive, constraining and rewarding instruments which keep the bondsman in thrall. The bondsman working on things does not completely overcome their thingness since they do not become what he wishes them to be, or not for himself. It is the Lord who reaps the enjoyment from the bondsman's labours.
>
> – Hegel 1998: 521-22

> The truth of independent self-consciousness is, therefore, to be found rather in the bondsman's self-consciousness than in the Lord's. Each is therefore the inverse of what it immediately and superficially is given as being. – Ibid.: 522

> The bondsman has the further advantage that in working on the object he as it were preserves his labour, makes the outward thing his own and puts himself into it. Where as the Lord's dealings with the object end in vanishing enjoyments. The bondsman overcomes the otherness and mere existence of material thinghood more thoroughly than the Lord and so achieves a more genuine self-consciousness. – Ibid.

> Hegel thinks that the discipline of service and obedience is essential to self-consciousness; mere mastery of things alone would not yield it. Only the discipline of service enables the conscious being in master himself, i.e. his finite, contingent, natural self. Without this discipline formative ability would degenerate into a narrow cleverness placed at the service of personal self-will. – Ibid.

Freedom of Self-consciousness

The freedom of self-consciousness takes place when it appeared as conscious manifestation in the history of spirit, which is called stoicism (Hegel 1998: 121).

> Its principle is that consciousness is a being that *thinks*, and that consciousness holds something to be essentially important or true and good only insofar as it *thinks* it to be such. – Hegel 1998: 121

It is further observed:

> While stoicism is the freedom which always comes directly out of bondage and returns into the pure universality of thought. As a universal form of the Worldspirit, stoicism could only appear on the scene in a time of universal fear and bondage, but also a time of universal culture which had raised itself to the level of thought.
>
> – Hegel 1998: 121

However, the freedom of self-consciousness is indifferent to natural existence. In this context it is stated:

> Freedom in thought has only *pure thought* as its truth, a truth lacking the fullness of life. Hence freedom in thought too is only the notion of freedom, not the living reality of freedom itself. For the essence of that freedom is at first only thinking in general, the form as such (of thought), which has turned away from the independence of things and returned into itself. But since individuality in its activity should show itself to be alive, or in its thinking should grasp the living world as a system of thought.
>
> – Ibid.: 122

Puruṣa (Self-conscious Human Being) in the Sāṁkhya–Yoga of Indian Philosophy

The *Puruṣa* is equated with the seer (i.e. *draṣṭā*), which in turn is nothing but pure consciousness. Although it is pure, it appears to see through the mind. It has been emphasized that the

> *Puruṣa* according to the Yogic philosophy is the Ultimate Reality hidden behind the phenomenal world in its subjective aspect.
>
> – Taimni 1999: 185-86

However, it has been clearly stated that

> not until the last vehicle has been transcended consciousness can be known in its purity. That is the *Puruṣa*, the real *draṣṭā*.
>
> – Ibid.: 187

Similar observation has been made in *Sāṁkhya-Kārikā* 19 of Īśvarakṛṣṇa, in which it is stated that the *Puruṣa* is pure witness, neutral spectator and non-agent (Swami Virupakshananda 2003: 61).

The *Puruṣa* is also defined negatively as eternal and indivisible "without variableness or shadow of turning" as resting ever in its own pure self-identity. It is deprived even of ideal activity and it becomes just the possibility of a pure consciousness (Radhakrishnan 2002: 320-21).

However, the *Puruṣa* can be inferred on various grounds referred to in *Sāṁkhya-Kārikā* 17. These grounds are (Swami Virupakshananda 2003: 55):

1. *Saṁghāta-parārthātvāt* which means that all composite objects exist for the sake of someone other than themselves.
2. *Triguṇādi-viparyāyāt* that the *Puruṣa* is opposite to what is constituted by the three *guṇas*.
3. *Adhiṣṭhānāt* that the inanimate objects are in the need of being controlled by some conscious principle.
4. *Bhoktṛbhāvāt* that there must be an experiencer-conscious principle.
5. *Kaivalyārtham* that man tries to attain the absolute freedom from the worldly affairs which are often resulting into sorrow, pain, etc.

Having inferred the *Puruṣa* on the above grounds, it is stated that the *Puruṣa* or the self may be known immediately in its reflection (Bhattacharyya 1983: 192). Since the *Puruṣa* is nothing but pure consciousness, it has to reflect mainly through the instrument of mind. As a result, the essential nature of pure consciousness (i.e. *Puruṣa*) cannot be known so long it identifies with the mind which happens to be the object of consciousness. But it is equally important that *Puruṣa* (self) cannot experience anything without the mind. This is evident from the following comment:

> The self having been reflected in the mind (*buddhi*) and identified with it, appears to possess knowledge, pleasure, etc.

> which actually subsist in the mind. It means thereby that it is the reflection of self in the mind which appears to experience pleasure, pain, etc. while, in fact, they are modes of mind only. ... The self appears to take on the characteristics of mind in which it has reflected. ... This is what is traditionally known as theory of single reflection. – Ram 1995: 110

As against the theory of single reflection, Vijñānabhikṣu proposed double reflection. It is stated:

> Just as there is a reflection of *buddhi* in the self, so there is a reflection of the self in *buddhi* also, otherwise the self's experience would not be possible. – Sinha 1958: 235

This double reflection seems to be self-contradictory in the sense that how it is possible to know the self,

> if the self knows itself through the reflection, in itself, of the mental mode which assumes the form of the self. – Ibid.

In this context, Vijñānabhikṣu says:

> There is no contradiction in the cognition of self by the self inasmuch as the self is essentially self-luminous and, hence it can be both, the illuminating agent and the illumined object, the knowing subject as well as the known object. – Ibid.

Vijñānabhikṣu further observes:

> Though there is no real difference in the nature of self, yet we may distinguish the self in its pure essence, as the original (*bimba*) from the reflection of the mental mode in the self, as an image of the self (*pratibimba*). Of these two aspects of the self, which is the knowing subject and which is the known object. Vijñānabhikṣu holds that the self as determined by the mental mode, which is modified into the form of the self as the knowing subject and the self in its pure essence free from all determinations, is known as object. – Ibid.: 235

Yet, the theory of double reflection of Vijñānabhikṣu has some basic problems. In the context, it is stated:

> The law of parsimony also favours the view of single reflection as the acts of perception, knowledge, etc. can be explained adequately with the help of this theory. In the Sāṁkhya philosophy, the effect in a sense is identical with the cause. In this case, the reflecting of the self is the effect of the original self. Therefore, the acts of perception, knowledge, etc. which appear to belong to the reflection can also be taken to belong to the original self. – Ram 1995: 110-11

It may be pointed out that the double reflection theory of Vijñānabhikṣu has been amended by K.C. Bhattacharyya through the dual function of mind reflected in the self. Let us see how it works. In reflection, the mind plays dual functions:

i. The mind while reflecting the object, it gets modalized into substantial *vr̥tti* similar to the object. The *vr̥tti* of *buddhi* appears as the self-reflecting object. This has been referred to as the outward grades of objective substance and characterized as causal manifestation (Bhattacharyya 1983: 158).

ii. While manifesting the object, the mind functions non-causally. In this case, the mind does not go into any substantial transformation as has been the case in the functioning *vr̥tti*. This is known as the mental mode of subjective function of *bhāva*, without which no object can become an object of knowledge (Ram 1995: 123).

However, these two functions are illusorily referred to the self (ibid.: 124).

This illusionary character has been assigned to the reflection of the self in *buddhi-bhāva* mainly with a view to show that it is in conformity with the Sāṁkhya view that

> the self is known as what mind is not as it is known in *viveka* (*bhāva* – the subjective knowing function of the mind), which implies a mental mode of the form "I am I". It means that *bhāva* is a state of the mind superior to *vr̥tti*, which happens to give rise

> to the former, the subjective function of the mind in which the self is known as what mind is not in the final stage of meditation.
>
> – Ram 1995: 125

The above form of distinguishing a substantial function of mind from its non-substantial, non-causal function known as *bhāva* seems to have provided an improvement over Vijñānabhikṣu's theory of double reflection.

Self-Conscious Being in Advaita Vedānta

It is stated:

> The only direct cognition, in the strict sense, in pure consciousness manifests within each and every individual as the luminous self.
>
> – Swami Satprakashananda 2001a: 90

This has been again repeated by stating that "*Brahman* is manifest in every human being as self-awareness that is direct and intuitive" (ibid.: 91). This is explained below:

> This is immutable consciousness (*kūṭastha*) ever present as the witness self (*sākṣī*). It illumines the mental states: pleasure, pain, hope, fear, knowledge, ignorance, love, hate, memory, loss of memory and so forth. The mental states are immediately cognized because of their presence to witness self. It is the immediacy of self-awareness that makes an object immediately known. To be directly cognized, an object must be allied with luminous self. Knowledge is direct, i.e. perceptual, when the object is known directly. The immutable consciousness that the witness self is, being reflected in the mind and apparently limited by it, appears as the ego, the empirical self, which functions as the percipient (*pramātā*). So the percipient is inseparable from the witness self, its basis.
>
> – Ibid.

The above description of immutable consciousness, self-awareness (self-consciousness) refers to individual self (*jīvātman*). We are treating individual self as a self-conscious being.

However, there is a difference regarding the *jīva* (individual self) between the two post-Śaṅkara Advaita schools: Vivaraṇa and Bhāmatī. The former defines the *jīva* as a reflection of *Brahman* (i.e. pure consciousness), whereas the latter refers to *jīva* as *Brahman* limited by ignorance. The view of Vivaraṇa is known as Pratibimbavāda. It is also referred to as *cidābhāsa*, whereas the view of Bhāmatī is known as Avacchedavāda (theory of limitation). Both the views are stated below.

Vivaraṇa School of Vedānta

The individual self has been defined as the reflection of *Brahman* (pure consciousness) due to the organ of egoity acting as a limited adjunct (*upādhi*) (Thibaut 1994: 136, v. XXXI). Further, a distinction is added by the fact that the individual self in dreamless sleep is particularized by nescience (ignorance) in general.

The following commentary on *Vivaraṇaprameya Saṁgraha* XXXII is worth stating:

> The self – although in reality is nothing else, but pure consciousness and of an altogether non-objective character – insofar as reflected in the organ of Egoity superimposed upon it (the Self) becomes capable of relating itself to that sphere of thought and speech which is connoted by the word "I", and thus presenting itself to consciousness as fused with organ of Egoity – which is superimposed upon the Self in the "I", consciousness – itself is thought and spoken of, in a derived or metaphorical sense, as the object of this "I" consciousness. It is in this way that the superimposition of the "I" on the Self shows itself to be possible.
>
> – Thibaut 1994: 140

It may, however, be stated that consciousness as reflected in finite *ajñāna* (ignorance) and identified with mind is the empirical self, the ego, *jīva-caitanya*, the doer of actions and experiencer of their fruits (*kartā-bhoktā*). This functions as the cognizer (*pramātā*). Being subject to *ajñāna*, it ascribes to itself various psychical and physical conditions. It is also called *cidābhāsa* (the reflected self) (Swami Satprakashananda 2001a: 83).

Bhāmatī School of Vedānta

According to the Bhāmatī school, the self as pure consciousness is in conformity with scripture, traditional codes, epics and Purāṇas. It is by nature pure, conscious and liberated. The reality of the self consists in its uncontradictable self-luminosity. The very nature of the self happens to be as consciousness. The reality is not anything different from that (Sastri and Raja 1992: 23).

When the self as conscious gets united with the complex of gross and subtle bodies and the organs, it acquires the power to act and enjoy.

> Though self manifest, yet by intermixture with the objects like intellect, etc. it somehow becomes the object of the concept "I", the substrate of "I"ness and is (variously) designated *jīva*, creature (*jantu*) or the knower of the field (*kṣetrajña*). – Ibid.: 41

The *jīva* is, however, not different from the self as consciousness. Yet, it is made by the concept "I" and for empirical usage it is treated as the agent and enjoyer. It has been further explained that "the *jīva* becomes an object if there is superimposition he becomes an object" (Sastri and Raja 1992: 41). This is mainly because the process of becoming is beginningless like the seed and the sprout. In this argument, there is no self-contradictory circularity involved because each subsequent superimposition takes for its object the previous superimposition and its impressions they have left (ibid.). It may, however, be stated that the *jīva* is not an object, as non-different from the self as consciousness. Yet, it becomes an object because of its conditioned form (ibid.). In the context of the *jīva* as an object of the ego notion, the following observation may be worth noting:

> The *Bhāmatī* explains the ego-notion as figurative, using the form "somehow". The effect of this is to weaken the force of the words in Śrī Śaṅkara's commentary. "But it (the self) is not altogether a non-object, since it is the object of ego-notion." This passage in Śrī Śaṅkara's commentary is an answer to the objection "How

> could an object be superimposed on something that is not an object?" One should only say of the Self, he replies, that it is not the object of the notion "you": it is not right to say that it is not an object in any sense whatever. For here the words of the commentary accept that the self is the object of notion "I". Note also that the opponent is not here made to raise the difficulty of how the Self could be a knowing subject having the notion of "I" for its object – nor is anything said by the exponent of the finally accepted view to dispel this difficulty. – Alston 1997: 59

However, the inner self appears to be delimited by the mind and other organs. This works as both an object and a subject at the same time. As a result, the *jīva* performs the action and enjoys its experiences. This is supported by twofold ignorance as the effect and cause, the substratum of the ego sense (Sastri and Raja 1992: 59).

Relation between the Absolute and the Individual Self

According to Vācaspati Miśra, relation between the Absolute and the individual self is:

> The universal consciousness, which is the object (*viṣaya*) of nescience, is *Īśvara*, and the same consciousness, which is the abode (*āśraya*) of nescience, is an empirical self. He admits many nesciences, which abide in many *jīvas*. Many individual souls are the abodes of many individual nesciences, (*tulā-vidyā*). But one *Īśvara* is the object of all nesciences. The world appearances differ in different individual souls because of their different nesciences. An individual soul itself is conditioned or limited by its nescience is the material cause of its world appearance. – Sinha 1971: 221

This limitation (*avaccheda*) concept of the individual soul may be supported by Madhusūdana Sarasvatī's approach in defining the *jīva*. He has adopted a twofold approach:

1. Image consciousness (*bimba-caitanya*) concealed by ignorance is *Īśvara* and consciousness as counter-image (*pratibimba*) in ignorance is *jīva*, or
2. pure consciousness not concealed (*anupahita*) by ignorance is

Īśvara and the consciousness concealed by ignorance is *jīva* (Timalsina 2006: 127-28).

The *jīva* being delimited by the internal organ, it becomes a knower of limited objects which come into contact with the internal organ through the eyes, etc. As a result, the *jīva* becomes the experiencer of many things (Swami Gambhirananda 2007: 509).

However, there is a difference between Madhusūdana Sarasvatī and Vācaspati: The former believes in Ekajīvavāda (one soul in all human beings), whereas the latter has proposed Anekajīvavāda (many individual souls). In order to justify one soul in all human beings, it is stated:

> Since all the respective differences can be explained on the basis of differences themselves of internal organs, which are the repositories of happiness, sorrow, etc. therefore, there is no valid proof of the multiplicity of the self, which is changeless and illuminator of all, because it permeates everything through its nature as Existence and Self-effulgence.
>
> – Swami Gambhirananda 2007: 87

It may, however, be mentioned that the individual self (i.e. *jīvātman*) is also known as the witness self. In this conext, the witness consciousness explained is as follows.

Witness Consciousness

It has been observed that the witnessing consciousness does not perform any action and hence it is not an enjoyer or a sufferer. In that, it is mainly a disinterested onlooker (Bhattacharyya 2004: 70). This witnessing approach has been adopted mainly to show that

> witnessing consciousness witnesses not merely what the individual does in his waking state but also dream state and also the dreamless sleep. The consciousness that is aware of the "blank" of dreamless cannot be ordinary experience of objects. Witnessing consciousness, which cannot go to sleep, is there to "know" the state of sleep. – Ibid.: 71

The above observations resemble the deep-sleep experience of the Advaita Vedānta. In the deep sleep, pure consciousness persists, as a result when one wakes up from sleep one immediately remembers that, "I slept well and I do know anything". This shows that remembering of the sleep experience becomes possible mainly because of the persistence of pure consciousness in deep sleep.

It may, however, be stated that the *ālaya-vijñāna* of the Yogācāra has been referred to as the soul in disguise and compared with the *Ātman* of the Advaita Vedānta. There are substantial differences between the two. Yet, on point of ego there is an agreement. It has been observed that the *ālaya* represents a stage where the sense of ego has not arisen.

> The closest parallel to this conception in the Brāhmanical systems is that of the *sākṣī* in Advaita Vedānta. The *sākṣī* is pure consciousness as covered by indeterminate ignorance (*avidyāvacchinna*) and is sharply distinguished from the empirical subject (*pramātā*). Consciousness has not yet been individualized by mind (*antaḥkaraṇa*).
>
> – Chatterjee 1999: 97

Pure consciousness has been used as witness consciousness in the Advaita Vedānta. This happens to be the knower of three states of consciousness: deep sleep, dream and waking. However, there is no difference between the *Ātman* and *sākṣī* (witness) according to Śaṅkarācārya. It may be stated that later on a distinction between the two has been made.

Dharmarāja Adhvarīndra in the *Vedānta-Paribhāṣā* has made a distinction between the *Ātman* and *sākṣī*. Pure consciousness (eternal consciousness) is referred to as the *Ātman*. When it is limited by the mind (*antaḥkaraṇa*), it becomes, the *jīva* (individual self). But when pure consciousness has the mind as its limiting adjunct (*upādhi*), it becomes the *sākṣī* (witness consciousness). In the case of *jīva*, the mind is a qualifying attribute (*viśeṣaṇa*). Whereas in the case of *sākṣī*, the mind is a limiting adjunct (*upādhi*) (Swami Madhavananda 2000: 37-38).

However, the Vedānta has recognized two orders of Reality: the transcendental and the empirical; the former is the Absolute and the latter is the relative. It may be noted that from the empirical plane being the experience of duality, the absolute reality of non-dual may be difficult to know. Yet, it is not beyond experience, as is evident from the following observation:

> Being the Reality and the source of all phenomena, it is not an entity beyond experience. It is the inner self (*pratyak-ātman*) of all, the eternal Subject. It is self-cognized within phenomena; that is, it is intuitively cognized, directly and immediately, as the Pure Witness Self (*sākṣī*) within by all beings. It is the Ground and Source of all objective experience, internal or external, on the phenomenal plane, just as one is aware of one's eyes without seeing them, for they enable one to see all things. This is the noumenal point of view. All phenomena are revealed by, and get their validity from the Self, which is Pure Witness Subject in all.
>
> – Swami Mukhyananda 2006: 49-50

The pure witness subject is nothing but pure consciousness which one may get by abstracting from empirical consciousness all the limitations like mind and matter. In that, it becomes mindless and bodiless (i.e. removing involvement of consciousness in material things) consciousness (Woodroffe 2001: 303). This pure consciousness is treated as the Absolute Reality, which in turn is referred to as *Brahman* or *Ātman* in Advaita Vedānta. It may be explained by taking the instance of an individual human being who never exists a moment without thinking about his plan of work in the mind to actualize it. In fact, every human being searches constantly

> for the new avenues of self-expression, so that one can actualize for oneself the self content of happiness. By extension of the farthest limit, what is true for the individual is also true for the Absolute Reality. – Prasad 1994: 137

The existence of consciousness lies in the never-ending functional states of its manifestation. In every functional state, it attains a new form. It takes numerous forms. In fact, it is stated:

> There is no actual state in which consciousness is functionless. Unmanifest consciousness, as reality behind all the functional states, is only a verticalized version, or an abstraction. When the same is seen horizontally it appears as the manifest world. What is called creation here is only the process by which the vertical or abstract Reality becomes horizontalized and attains a manifest form. It is nothing other than the unfoldment of the endless creative urge inherent in the Self or Consciousness.
>
> – Prasad 1994: 138

1

Are Particles Conscious?

THE following scientific observations are most intriguing:

> The particles "sees" the experimenter, who observes the hole through which the particle passes, and "behaves" accordingly. This experimenter always sees a particle passing through one hole or the other, never both at once. If an arrangement is made to record the specific hole through which the particle passes, the pattern that builds up the detector screen does not show any trace of interference. This means that the particle has passed through one hole or the other but not through both the holes. *The particles are conscious of two things* (italics are mine). They know whether or not both holes are open. They also know whether or not any observer is watching them. They not only know, but also adjust their behaviour accordingly. This provides the clearest example of the interaction of the observer with experiment.
>
> – Panda 2008: 112

Now the question is that whether the electron and the proton have mind through which consciousness manifests according to Vedānta of Indian philosophy. This may, further, be clarified by the observation that all conscious states only exist,

> as experienced by mind or animal subject and in that sense it has subjective or first-person ontology.

Therefore, it may be said that if the electron and the proton are not having mind, they are certainly not conscious.

When physicists try to explain the result of double-slit experiment of yong, taking for granted that light behaves as particles, they are confronted with a similar problem. Photons behave unpredictably like "conscious" electrons of Feynman's two-hole experiment (Swami Jitatmananda 1993: 24).

Thought Experiment

Thought experiments are the most important modes of exploration in physics. This is explained below:

i. Thought experiments are laboratory experiments of the mind in which physicists explore the imagination so as to tease information out of nature. Thought experiments are experiments that are thought about rather than performed, although sometimes they can be performed too. In a thought experiment no hands get dirty, but minds can become clarified. Einstien himself often used thought experiments as a way of attaining insight into the nature of things. Wheeler himself was considered to be a master of thought experiments, extrapolating them in the most extreme fashion imaginable (Levy 2019: 270-71).

ii. Thought experiments are expressions of profundity and power of our imagination to help us find our place in the universe, and they indicate that the nature of the universe is more thought like than is generally acknowledged (ibid.: 271).

In the quantum physics, David Bohm has defined thought in essence as the active response to the memory in every phase of life. Thought includes the intellectual, emotional, sensuous, muscular and physical response to memory.

> To treat separately makes for fragmentation and confusion. All these are one process of response of memory to each actual situation, which response in turn leads to a further contributor to memory, thus conditioning the next thought. – Bohm 2012: 64

It is further, clarified that "thought is basically a material process" (ibid.: 66).

However, one of the most difficult and subtle point about the question is that what is relationship between the convent of thought and process of thinking which produces the content. This is explained below:

> A major source of fragmentation is indeed the generally accepted presupposition that the process of thought is sufficiently separate from and independent of its content, to allow us generally to carry out clear, orderly, rational thinking, which can properly judge this content as correct or incorrect, rational or irrational, fragmentary or whole, etc. Actually, as has been seen, the fragmentation involved in a self-world view is not only in the content of thought, but in the general activity of the person, who is doing thinking, and thus, it is as much in the process of thinking as it is in the content. Indeed, content and process are not two separately existent things, but rather, they are two aspects of view of one whole movement. Thus fragmentary content and fragmentary process have to come to an end together.
>
> – Bohm 2012: 23

The above observation may be resolved easily in thinking itself. This is because thinking is thinking of something, which is nothing but its contents. It is further stated that the thinking contains both the observer and the objects (i.e. content of thinking). Both became one mainly because the self-consciousness is embodied in human being. This is the Vedāntic interpretation. Now let us see how the observer and the objects are explained by David Bohm (2018: 79-80).

i. The observer is what gathers: it selects and gathers the relevant information and organizes it into some meaning and picture. And that is what is done by the assumptions in thought. According to what you assume, you collect and gather certain information as important and put it together in a certain way, in a certain structure. Therefore, the assumptions are functioning as a kind of *observer*. When we observe we forget that and we are looking without taking that into account. But this "observer" profoundly affects what it is observing and is also affected by what is observing – there is really very little separation between them. If the emotions are what are being observed, then the "observing" assumptions are profoundly affected by the emotions and the emotions are profoundly affected by the assumptions. On the other hand, if you say the emotions are the observer and are determining the way things are organized, then the assumptions will be observed. Either way, the observed is profoundly affected by the observer and the observer by the observed – they are one cycle, one process. The separations between them is not very significant.

ii. If on the other hand, I observe a chair on the other side of the room, what is going on in me is not very much affected by the chair; and what is going on in the chair is not profoundly affected by me. We could say in that case that the observer is significantly different from the observed. But when looking at your emotions or looking at your thought, that cannot be the case. Similarly, when looking at societies or looking at another person, what you see depends on your assumptions, and you will get an emotional reaction from that person which enters you and effects the way you see.

iii. Therefore, at certain stage, the distinction between the observer and the observed cannot be maintained, or as Krishnamurti used to say, *the observer is observed*. If you do not put the two together, the observer and the observed – if you do not put the assumptions together with the emotions – then the whole thing will be wrong. If I say I am going to look into my mind, but do not consider my assumptions, then the picture is wrong *because the assumptions are looking*. That is a common problem of introspection. You say "I am going to look myself inwardly", but the assumptions are not looked at the assumptions are looking.

Two-Hole Experiment

When physicists try to explain the result of double-slit experiment of Yong, taking for granted that light behaves as particles, they are confronted with a similar problem. Photons behave unpredictably like the "conscious" electrons of Feynman's two-hole experiment (Swami Jitatmananda 1993: 24).

It may, however, be stated that in explaining the two-hole experiment (double-slit experiment) does not require a tiny intelligent being, what is required is the understanding of the concept of "small" and "big" objects as defined by the new physics. This is explained below:

> Light quanta, electrons, and atoms are small objects. An orange is a large object. But in comparison to the earth an orange is very small: as small as an atom is compared to an orange. *What the new physics does is to give an absolute meaning to the concept of "small" and "big" objects.* An object is small in the absolute sense if the effect of the "disturbance" which inevitably accompanies an act of observation is not negligible. A certain indeterminate disturbance is inevitable even under *ideal* conditions, that is, observations made with "perfect instruments" supposed to be free of all limitations except what are inherent in the very nature of things. If disturbance has negligible effect on the state of the object, the object is said to be in the absolute sense. The moon is a big object because looking at it, observing its motion, has no effect on the motion. An electron, or an atom, is a small object in the absolute sense, because the unavoidable disturbance (inherent in an act of observation) drastically alters the state under observation. Note that a perfect observation is imaginary observation with ideally "perfect" instruments. It is a "thought experiment". The only requirement for it is that it should be theoretically permissible. It should conform to the laws of physics. *Ideal experiments are useful tools of thought.* A certain indeterminate disturbance accompanying an observation, totally unpredictable, is inherent in the very nature of things. Nature is made that way. It is a direct consequence of the existence of the Planck's constant. To appreciate the absolute distinction between big and small systems is the gateway to modern physics.
>
> – Kothari 2002: 309

However, every electron goes through all the slits. This situation is altogether inconceivable. In this context, the following observation in worth stating:

> How can an electron, the same electron, cross through a number of slits at the same time? Impossible! How can the same electron be at the same time? You and I cannot pass through two doors at the same time; yet the photons and electrons do that as if it were a normal thing for them. What is the reason? It is none other than the fact that photons, electrons, atoms are small objects – small in the absolute sense; and you and I are big objects in the absolute sense. The small objects judged by the behaviour of big ones, perform literally miracles. – Ibid.: 310-11

It may, further, be mentioned:

> The electron is moving in the form or guise of a "wave" – *a wave of probability amplitude.* These waves are not in physical sense, not in our everyday space, but in an abstract mathematical space. That can have many dimensions [If the electron wave were in physical space, we could see it – but we don't. A photon or an electron, has a dual aspect; a wave aspect and a particle aspect]. The two aspects are complimentary. The one aspect excludes the other aspect. That is why the two aspects are not contradictory. A contradiction between them could arise only if the two aspects could be observed at the same time. But this never happens; and we have compelling theoretical arguments that this could not happen. The wave and the particle aspects are complementary and not contradictory. – Ibid.: 311

It has been further explained:

> At the root of the wave-particle duality is *the principle of absolute indistinguishability, absolute identities of particles of the same kind.* All electrons in the universe are absolutely identical, absolutely indistinguishable from one another. – Ibid.: 313

In the total wave function, the identity of individual electron is completely lost. There is no separate individuality of electron in the total wave function. This is explained as follows:

> *The electrons have submerged themselves, as it were in one "brotherhood" of electrons.* The Many have become One ... when we speak of the total-wave-function or the field, and the many identical particles incorporated in the wave function, it is not sort of an aggregate, a sum of the Many. In an aggregate, the Oneness is no more than an euphemism for the Many that are still visible, may be dimly in the aggregate. The concept of Oneness in quantum mechanics is a totally, fundamentally, new concept. ... The One is an abstract space, the Many in physical space. Two aspects are complementary (emphasis added by italics).
>
> – Kothari: 314

Wave–Particle Duality

It is observed:

> The ambiguous spatio-temporal and dynamic features of quantum particles are often expressed in terms of *wave-particle duality* whereas some philosophers of science have stated that this is obsolete, in quantum physics wave-particle duality is quite a current concept.
>
> Wave–particle duality is an informal concept. It does not belong to any specific quantum theory.
>
> In a certain sense, the concept of wave–particle duality bridges the gap between the probabilistic interpretation and the individual subatomic processes which happen in the measurement devices. We will see that this is partially due to Born's probabilistic interpretation of the quantum mechanical wave function and partially due to Bohr's complementarity interpretation of individual quantum phenomena. – Falkenburg 2007: 265

Bohr's Complementarity View

The following observations are worth noting regarding the complementarity view of wave–particle duality:

> Bohr's como lecture of 1927 expressed wave–particle duality in terms of complementarity. This concept became a cornerstone of the Copenhagen interpretation of quantum mechanics. (According

> to Howard 2002, however, what is today called the Copenhagen interpretation is due to Heisenberg, whereas Bohr's own view is just the complementarity view.) In order to understand what it means, we have to take a step back to the operational content of the Planck–Einstein and Einstein–de Broglie relations $E = hu$ and $p = hk$. They were confirmed by quantum phenomena such as particle tracks and energy-momentum conservation in the compton effect vs the diffraction patterns generated by light rays and electron beams. – Falkenburg 2007: 212

> Bohr called such phenomena *complementary.* His complementarity view of quantum mechanics is based on the correspondence principle. According to this, complementary quantum phenomena correspond to *classical* concepts or models of the phenomena which *mutually exclude and complement each other.* Bohr thought a full understanding of quantum phenomena is only possible in terms of corresponding classical concepts and models. According to him, the experimental conditions under which particle tracks and scattering events are observed are complementary to the conditions under which interference fringes appear. – Ibid.: 272

Bohr's concept of complementarity changed over time. From the very beginning, however, it embraced several conceptual levels. (A careful analysis is found in Scheibe 1971: 29-35. See also Folks 1985; Meyer-Abich 1965; Murdoch 1981. Greenstein and Zajone 1997 give a short systematic account in the context of quantum optics.) Only in his later writings did Bohr make it explicit that mutually exclusive experimental devices generate complementary phenomena. This seems to be the last conceptual stage. In the famous Como lecture, Bohr introduced the concept as follows:

> The very nature of the quantum theory thus forces us to regard the space–time coordination and the claim of causality, the union of which characterizes the classical theories as complementary but exclusive feature of the description (Bohr 1929: 90).
>
> – Falkenburg 2007: 272-73

The neutron has a greater mass than proton. This makes it possible that this type of decay can happen. The energy of the proton + electron + neutrino together is still less than the energy of neutron. Consequently, the decay products take momentum out of the interaction. The other way around, a proton turning into a neutron is not possible, since the neutron is lighter. It would require catching an energetic W-boson making an up quark change into a down quark. Since the weak interaction is already so short ranged and W-bosons are not abundantly around, the change for to happen is astronomically small for a free proton.

– Ibid.: 238-39

2

Space and Time

Introduction

Space and time have become enigmas in Indian philosophy mainly due to two main reasons:

i. The views about space and time have been varying quite sharply in different systems of Indian philosophy. The Vaiśeṣika school has treated space and time as two different realities. Whereas in Sāṁkhya and Vedānta, space and time have only relative existence. According to Vedānta, space and time are the forms of experience but they are not ultimates. The real is obscured by them (Radhakrishnan 2002: 562). Newton has, however, postulated space and time as absolute realities. Space was always at rest, infinite, indefinite and eternal. Further, according to Newton, time was eternal without beginning and end (Panda 2008: 17). The position is quite different in the case of Einstein, who treated space and time as relative existence. Einstein conceived space and time as continuum (ibid.: 375). Space is not independent of time and vice versa. But the combinations of both (space and time) form one relative existence referred to as space-time. Advaita Vedānta has also conceived space and time as one relative existence long back. This is mainly due to the fact that Vedānta has accepted only pure consciousness as the Absolute Reality referred to as *Brahman* from which the entire universe (including time and space) becomes objective appearance, which has only relative existence.

ii. It is a well-known fact that sense perception does not depend only on the sense organs but it also requires the mind which forms the image of the object through which it is being cognized. The objects, while striking the sense organ, create the sensations which spring up in the mind, resulting thereby into the cognition of the objects. It may be stated that the mind always works in the shadow of past, because it is the repository of the *saṁskāras* (dispositions) of all the experiences which it has throughout the course of successive lives. These *saṁskāras* influence the mind to form its own image to see the object. As a result, the true nature of object existing in the space is not known. However, it does not mean that the objects do not exist, it only means that

> they are not what they seem to be. They are the products of our mind, depending upon the formation of mental images in our mind and their rapid succession as different kinds of forces play upon the mind. – Taimni 2005: 340

In this context, it is observed that, "according to the occult doctrine, both time and space are illusions" (ibid.: 336).

In the case of time, the problem happens to be quite different in the sense that the empty time cannot be perceived. It is known mainly through events. "Time might be thought to exist in relation to things" (Murti 2003: 199). In that, it is known only by human being, "who has an awareness of time" (Organ 1988: 77). This is evident from an observation that "one consciousness being viewing itself in extension, subjectively as Time, objectively as Space" (Aurobindo 2001: 144). Time has been explained in another way quite sharply by the fact that

> time is in me and I am in time. The container is at the same time the contained. I contain time, but time also contains me.
> – Chatterjea et al. 2014: 85

The theory of relativity as propounded by Einstein also supports the above observation related to time. It is stated:

> Each observer must have his own measure of time, as recorded by a clock carried with, and that identical clocks carried out by different observers would not necessarily agree.
>
> – Hawking 1988: 21

This shows that the theory of relativity has brought an end to the idea of absolute time. This has been reassured by the following recent observation:

> Einstein's theory of relativity has brought about a drastic change in our concepts of space and time. It has forced us to abandon the classical ideas of an absolute space as the stage of physical phenomena and of absolute time as a dimension separate from space. According to relativity theory, both space and time are relative concepts, reduced to the subjective role of elements of the language a particular observer uses to describe natural phenomena. To provide an accurate description of phenomena involving velocities close to the speed of light, a "relativistic" framework has to be used, one that incorporates time with the three space coordinates, making it a fourth coordinate to be specified relative to the observer. In such a framework space and time are intimately and inseparably connected and form a four-dimensional continuum called "space-time". In relativistic physics, we can never talk about space without talking about time and vice versa.
>
> – Capra and Luisi 2014: 76

Vaiśeṣika Philosophy

SPACE

Vaiśeṣika accepts the reality of space (*dik*). It makes distinction between space and *ākāśa*. The former is the general cause of all effects, whereas the latter happens to be the material cause of sound. *Ākāśa* is a substance (*bhūta-dravya*), while space (*dik*) is not (Panda 2008: 367). However, space is eternal and it is the cause of the notions of farness, nearness, etc. It is also unitary in the sense that it is spoken of as east, west, above, below, etc. (ibid.).

TIME

Time (*kāla*) is treated as an independent reality, whose function is to bring to things within the experience. It is substance which is the cause of our perceptions of simultaneity and succession, of slow and fast, of now and then (Acharya 1985: 62). However, the time happens to be responsible for the concrete changes of nature such as production, distinction and persistence of things (Radhakrishnan 2002: 191).

SPACE AND TIME

It is stated:

> Both space (*dik*) and time (*kāla*) are taken as the efficient causes of the entire universe in the Nyāya-Vaiśeṣika system. They are necessary common conditions in the production of effects.
>
> – Panda 2008: 367

However,

> the distinction between time and space is noticed in the Vaiśeṣika treatises. Space deals with coexistence, time with successions, or more accurately, space deals with visible objects, while time deals with things produced and destroyed. – Radhakrishnan 2002: 192

We have seen briefly how time and space have been defined in the Vaiśeṣika philosophy. In this context, it is important to discuss about the Vaiśeṣika atomic theory because, "it is space filled with atoms; it is also eternal and contains within itself the possibility of sound" (Acharya 1985: 59).

THE ATOMIC THEORY

In the development of a thing from the atomic up to the highest atomic state, there are four states:

i. atoms,
ii. molecules,
iii. inorganic compounds, and
iv. organic compounds.

In this context, the following observations are worth noting:

> At the outset we must understand that this question is not purely mechanical but chemical, biological, psychological and ethical as well, for at every step in the life of an atom a new factor comes into play. At first it is purely mechanical or dynamical, viz. vibration. Then comes the influence of heat which at once destroys the primary qualities of the atom and develops secondary qualities. By this heat, one is to understand both physical heat – the action of the *Teja* atom – as well as what is called animal heat. When the atom passes the stage of pure chemical action it comes under the influence of life – in other words what was atom becomes an organic substance informed with life. This "life" then comes under the direction of mind, and mind, again develops according to moral law. But life and mind do not grow out of atom; it is the influence of the conscious soul that brings life and mind in line with the molecular aggregate. – Acharya 1985: 51

THE ELEVEN MOMENTS THEORY

Thus, we see that

> at each step there is a change in the very nature of the substance, a change which we may say amounts to metamorphosis. This process is so rapid that we can only follow it with our mind. The stages we have noticed here can be understood on the analogy of the growth of the germ-plasm under the influence of body–heart or of a seed under the influence of solar heat. In the language of Vaiśeṣika doctors this process is called "the process of eleven moments".

It is given in Table 2.1:

Table 2.1: The Process of Eleven Moments

Stage Moment	*Changes*	*Occurred*
Chemical action: gradually increasing heat of *teja* atom	1st moment	Atomic change starting with the disintegration of the binary molecule.
	2nd moment	Loosening of the molecular cohesion in a compound substance.
	3rd moment	Dissolution of the molecule.
	4th moment	Disappearance of molecular qualities, e.g. colour (molecular colour, for instance, after the decomposition of the molecule cannot produce any photographic action; similarly the molecular sap cannot stimulate our nerve of taste or touch).
Beginning of atomic action	5th moment	The production of another quality. The atom is now in its original naked state, hence its original quality manifests itself.
	6th moment	Arrest of atomic reaction. Here the atomic action has reached, so to speak, its lowest ebb.
	7th moment	Now comes the guidance of conscious soul or spirit. After resting for a period of an infinitesimal fraction of a moment, atomic activity resumes its course.
Spiritual guidance	8th moment	Its character changes; the result of the contact of spirit with matter is mind and life, which now for the first time comes into line. In the case of man, germ and sperm-cell come into line with mind and soul. In the case of vegetable seed, a crude sensitive-ness is developed together with the power of assimilating all the nutritive elements derived from the soil, the air and the light. In the case of inorganic substances, a kind of energy arises which not only keeps all the particles together, but also accumulates fresh particles of a similar nature and thus the substance grows in volume or in height. The

Stage	*Moment*	*Changes Occurred*
		entering of this factor displaces the atoms. The whole group feels the pulsation of life, seeks more space, moves about, and thus becomes separated from its old surroundings. Along with the separation it is conjoined with a new position. It links itself to a new substance and in this way binary molecule is again produced.
Spiritual guidance (*continues*)	9th moment	Manifestation of atomic quality in the new binary molecules. The properties of the atoms now reappear under a new form in the developed compound substance. The physiology, for instance, with its nervous system and sensorium has now been formed. The senses, which are developed from the atoms, now respond to the stimuli of heat, light, taste, smell and touch. A stable compound substance has now been formed. Our expectation is that after developing this fully matured form the process will stop. As a matter of fact, atomic forces, life, mind and soul now stand in proper relation to each other – but other forces are at work, of which may be mentioned (a) the past moral history of the soul, (b) cosmic disturbances, and (c) disharmony between the inner series of mind, life and body. Hence a 10th stage may arise.
Cosmic action	10th moment	Immediately *after* the cessation of former process a new force may follow or come into play, or, *before* the completion of the ninth stage a new force may arise and change the direction or modify the grouping.
	11th moment	New division in the component whole may be caused leading to the formation of several new, independent parts.

Source: Acharya 1985: 52-54.

> One thing should be noticed here, viz. the self-renewing power of the substance at every moment. It is the nature of all activity to renew itself at every moment. – Acharya 1985: 54

FUNCTIONS OF DIFFERENT ATOMS

> This explanation, which is called Eleven Moments Theory, helps us to picture how intimately the chemical, physical, nervous and ethical properties displayed by things are bound up with the activity of their constituent atoms. We understand how the inherent instability of binary molecules prevents things from being permanent; they transform under heat and revert to a less and less unstable state. In this act of change a ray is shot out from the atom; it loses its structure and its parts; the succeeding atom is of a totally different complexion from its predecessor. – Ibid.

Atoms are eternal, ultimate, indivisible and infinitesimal. There are four kinds of atoms: earth, water, fire and air. These four classes of atoms produce four senses of touch, taste, sight and smell.

> *Ākāśa* has no atomic structure, and absolutely inert, being posited only as the substratum of sound, which is supposed to travel wave-like in the manifesting medium or vehicle of *vāyu* (air). Only the other four *bhūtas* unite (or disunite) in atomic or molecular forms. The orthodox view is that the presence of earth-atoms is necessary whenever chemical transformation under the operation of heat takes place. – Seal 1985: 99

However, atoms cannot exist in an uncombined state in creation, whereas atmospheric air is believed to be monoatomic in structure, i.e. to consist of masses of atoms in a loose uncombined state (ibid.).

The atoms may combine in one or other of the following ways:

1. One earth-atom, by an original tendency, unites with another to form a binary molecule. In the same way binary molecules of other *bhūtas* are formed. The atoms are processed of an inherent *parispanda* (rotary or vibratory motion), and when they unite in pairs, *so long as there is no chemical operation under the action of heat corpuscles*, the original qualities of atoms

produce homogeneous qualities in the binary molecules (Seal 1985: 99-100).

2. *Chemical combination*: Chemical combination takes place either between two or more substances which are isometric modifications of the same *bhūta* or between substances which are modes of different *bhūtas* (ibid.: 103).

   i. *Mono-bhautika compounds:* The simplest compounds are mono-*bhautika* compounds. These are compounds of different substances, which are isomeric modes of the same *bhūta* (ibid.: 104).

      a. Mono-*bhautika* compounds of the first order: In this category,

         > under the impact or impulse of heat corpuscles, the substances in chemical contract break up into their atoms. These atoms are homogeneous, possessing only the original physical and chemical characters of the *bhūta* concerned. – Ibid.

      b. Mono-*bhautika* compounds of higher order.

         > Again mono-*bhautika* compounds of the first order may chemically combine to form higher compounds and as the ultimate *bhūta* substratum is the same, the process of decomposition and recomposition will be essentially the same as before. – Ibid.: 106

   ii. *Hetero-bhautika quasi compounds:* The Nyāya–Vaiśeṣika maintains that in the case of bi-*bhautika* (or poly-*bhautika*) compounds, which are only quasi-compounds, there is another kind of contact between the heterogeneous atoms of different *bhūtas*, which may be called dynamic contact, and is distinguished in its operations *upaṣṭambha, viṣṭambha* or *avaṣṭambha.* In some cases, it so happens that the atoms of different isomeric modes of the same *bhūta* do not chemically combine under the mere application of heat; they require to be surrounded (and "excited", "energized") by atoms of different *bhūtas*. For example, in the case of oils and fats, as well as of plant saps and fruit juices, the earth-atoms must be dissolved in water (*āpa*) and it is only when water atoms (*āpa*-atoms) congregate round the former that dynamic intra-atomic forces are set up, and the earth-atoms (with the water-atoms in dynamic contact) now take on peculiar infra-sensible characters (colours, tastes, smells) under the impact of the heat-corpuscles, and then, under further impact, fall into groupings or collocations (of a very peculiar nature, to be precisely explained) which determine the nature of the composite substance thus produced (Seal 1985: 109).

3. *Mixtures-like Solutions*: A solution (of an earth substance in *āpa*) is a physical mixture of a peculiar kind, from which evaporation (or precipitation) ordinarily sets the water free (ibid.: 112).

   Chemical Action and Heat: The operation of heat is of course universally implied in chemical combinations. Where the application of external heat is wanting, Vātsyāyana, the great doctor of the Nyāya, points to the operation of internal heat (ibid.: 113-14).

The above atomic theory has been formulated, "on purely metaphysical grounds and tried it to simplify the world to thought" (Radhakrishnan 2002: 194). An attempt has been made recently to establish relationship between the thought process (representing the self) and the atom. This is explained below.

THOUGHT PROCESS AND ATOM

The relationship between the thought and the atom has been explained by the fact that, in both, there are no intermediate stages. This is evident from the following observation:

> When an atom makes a transition, or a "jump" from one

> stationary state to another, the actual process cannot be visualized or even imagined. There are no intermediate stages. We cannot break down the process into its components: The entire process of transition from one state to another is a non-visualizable, unanalysable, unity. *It is indivisible.* Its parts cannot even be imagined. It is a "quantum jump", as we call it. The interesting thing is that there is an analogous situation for *thought processes.* As we "think" – in any sequence of thoughts – there is always a sudden, discontinuous jump from one thought to the next. We are not aware of all of any intermediate stages. If we were so aware, no thinking would be possible. There would be an almost infinite sequence of "sub-thoughts" between two thoughts, like an infinity of points between the two ends of a line. *Quantum jumps for thought appear to be as much a necessity for the conscious self as these are for the atom. This analogy between the self and the atom – and it is no more than an analogy* – suggests some interesting possibilities for the mind. – Kothari 2002: 298

A modern Indian thinker J. Krishnamurti has also equated thought with self. This is evident from the statement that

> thought is the self, thought is the word which identifies itself as the "me", and whatever level, high or low, the self is placed, it is still within the field of thought. – Krishnamurti 1992: 97

It is further stated that, "thought has created the thinker" (ibid.: 39). In this context, however, the following observation is worth noting:

> An action requires a substratum, which belongs to a different ontic category and also that a quale requires a substance that also is ontically different. Since thoughts are both qualia (*guṇa*) and acts (*kriyā*), they require the self as their supportive substance and the thinker. We note it as a ground of disagreement, then, that if substance ontology is accepted, thoughts cannot be thinkers.
> – Chakrabarti 2001: 75

The representation of self through thought process in the analogy of self with atom as mentioned above does not seem to be appropriate according to Advaita Vedānta. This is mainly due to the fact that

> Śaṅkara argues that it is impossible for us to know the self by means of thought, since thought itself is a part of the flux belonging to the region of non-self. ... Yet we cannot think away the self; for there is no consciousness or experience possible apart from it. – Radhakrishnan 2002: 476

In fact,

> consciousness being the very essence of self, it shines itself and its awareness becomes immediate and direct. But when it manifests through the instrumentality of mind, the idea of ego enters in the mode of thought. In this process, it becomes difficult to know the true nature of his own self, but one gets immediate awareness of his own existence as "I am". In this context, it may be stated that "I am" therefore "I think", and not "I think, therefore I am (*cogito ergo sum*)". – Swami Satprakashananda 2001a: 83

SELF AND ATOM IN VEDĀNTIC PERSPECTIVE

The analogy of self with an atom is also observed in Vedānta. It is stated:

> As the very being of the universe, pure existence is man's innermost self. What is innermost in an atom must be innermost in man. By realizing one's true self, one can realize that.
> – Swami Satprakashananda 2004: 170

This may be explained through the Vedāntic concept of the material universe, which contains both: cosmic and individual. The former known as the macrocosmic is in essence the same as the latter described as the microcosmic. "The cosmos and the individual are made of the same stuff and show the same pattern" (Swami Nikhilananda 2008: 83). Therefore, an inference may be drawn that the atom of material world may be experienced through the innermost self of human beings.

Philosophy of Sāṁkhya-Yoga

TIME

Time is defined as phenomenal changes, intuited by us in the empirical consciousness fall into a series, which the understanding conceives as order in time. In this context, it is stated:

> The Time series, then, is a schema of the understanding for representing the course of Evolution. The *schema* of the understanding supervenes on the phenomenal world as order in Time, and hence in the empirical consciousness the Time series appears to have an objective reality and to form a continuum.
>
> – Seal 1985: 19

It is further stated:

> Time is of one dimension. Two moments cannot coexist; neither does any series of moments exist in reality. Order in time is nothing but the relation of antecedence and sequence, between the moment that is and the moment that went just before. But only one moment, the present exists. The future and the past have no meaning apart from potential and sub-latent phenomena.
>
> – Ibid.: 20

According to Sāṁkhya:

> the divisions of time are nothing more than heuristic distinctions or limiting adjuncts. There is no need to posit a distinct entity called time. – Larson and Bhattacharya 1987: 309

It has, however, been pointed out by Vijñānabhikṣu that

> this does not amount to a denial of time. It means that Time has no real (or objective) existence apart from the "moment". But the latter is real, being identical with the unit of change in phenomena. But even this is real only for our empirical (relative) consciousness, which intuits the relation of antecedence and sequence into the evolving reals (*guṇas*) in the stage of empirical intuition.
>
> – Seal 1985: 21

The above observations clearly indicate that time in Sāṁkhya-Yoga philosophy has only relative existence. Time has no place in the evolutionary process in Sāṁkhya-Yoga philosophy (Panda 2008: 368).

SPACE

Space is also defined like time. It is stated:

> Space (*dik*) as the totality of position, or as an order of coexistent points, is wholly relative to the understanding, like order in time, being constructed on the basis of relations of position intuited by our empirical (or relative) consciousness. – Seal 1985: 21

However, space is treated in the Sāṁkhya philosophy as evolutes of *prakṛti*. "It is a modification (*vikṛti*) of *Prakṛti* (Nature). Being a product, it cannot be eternal" (Panda 2008: 368). Therefore, space too has only relative existence in Sāṁkhya–Yoga philosophy.

SPACE AND TIME

On the basis of the *Sāṁkhya-Pravacana-Sūtram Bhāṣya* of Vijñāna bhikṣu, the verse II.12 has been translated into English as follows:

> Space and time come from *ākāśa* and the *upādhi*s.

As a commentary on the above verse it is stated:

> It is *ākāśa* itself that, according to the distinction of this and that *upādhi* or external condition, is denoted by the terms of Space and Time. They are, therefore, included in *ākāśa*. – Sinha 2013: 245

It may, however, be noted that both space and time have only relative existence because both are limited by external conditions.

Advaita Vedānta

It may be mentioned at the outset that whatever has been stated in the Upaniṣads about space and time is acceptable to Vedānta. About the origin of space, it is stated:

> In various places in the Upaniṣads, we come across texts dealing with creation, etc. which seem to represent different schools of thought. Some mention the origin of space, while others do not.
> – Swami Gambhirananda 2000: 444

However, finally it is stated that, "space is a product of *Brahman*". In fact, *Brahman* is the creator of the entire universe, which includes space according to Vedānta (ibid.: 458).

Since space is known to be separate from earth, etc. it must be a product (ibid.: 454). In that, space is not eternal because it has beginning (Panda 2008: 371). Therefore,

> Space is a substance, subtle enough to hold macro-objects like the Earth and the Sun and macro-particles like the electron and the photon.
> – Ibid.: 371

In *Chāndogya Upaniṣad* IX.1, it is stated:

> For all things certainly originate from Space, and they merge by moving towards Space. For Space is certainly greater than all these. Space is their supreme goal.
> – Swami Gambhirananda 2003: 82

However, the following commentary on this verse is relevant here:

> Space strictly means that which gives room for everything to exist (*avakāśa dātr̥ akāśaḥ*). This "giving room to exist" may be construed as having two dimensions: one physical and the other metaphysical. *Ākāśa*, in the physical sense of space, provides room for all cosmic bodies. Even in the structure of an extremely minute atom, the space occupied by energy particles, compared to the empty space within it, it is quite insignificant. Even those particles, constituting its nucleus or orbiting it, are not confirmable either as matter or non-matter, either as entities or non-entities. That is to say, whether they are really physical or metaphysical is yet to be decided, perhaps never to be decided.
> – Prasad 2006a: 101

Taittirīya Upaniṣad II.1.1, however, describes space as the cosmogenical sequence.

> Space (*ākāśa*) was the first product from which hydrogen gas originated through generation of series of particles. The field of modern science is this *ākāśa*. Some scientists are of the opinion that space contains field. In such a notion, the void nature of

> space is still maintained. Advaita Vedānta says that space is field. Three subtle entities are recognized in Advaita Vedānta. These are the primeval waters (*āpaḥ, ka* or *ambhas*), *prāṇa* and space (*ākāśa, kha* or *aditi*). – Panda 2008: 371

On the above verse of the *Taittirīya Upaniṣad*, the following commentary is worth quoting. The sound has, however, happens to the quality of space:

> The same (*ākāśa*) in its abstract and epitomized form constitutes the sense organ of hearing in the individual. This is how ears have the capacity to contact sound. Basically the sense organ and the object sensed are constituted of the same element. By means of this particular kind of sense perception, the individual attains his or her identity with the universal. – Prasad 1994: 97

TIME

The objective existence of time has not been recognized by Advaita Vedānta. This is evident from *Māṇḍūkya Upaniṣad* II.14 in which it is stated that time is a mental construction generated by the occurrence of more than one event (Panda 2008: 372).

Brahman is the creator of time (*kāla-kāra*). This has the reference of *Śvetāśvatara Upaniṣad* VI.16. However, it is stated that

> the origin of conceptual time is simultaneous with the beginning of creation. There was no time before the cosmic egg appeared. There will also be no time after the phenomenal world is dissolved. – Ibid.

The concept of time can be understood better from the sleep experience in the Vedāntic framework. After awakening from sleep, one generally says that I have slept for so many hours. This indicates mainly the interval between two thoughts. Its implication for time is stated below:

> If we carefully consider the actual experience, we shall find that duration has no part in it: we experience duration only in states characterized by the succession of thoughts. Time is, therefore,

> the object of consciousness: time, in other words, has no existence unless we are thinking of it; and our concept of time is based on the ideas of past, present and future. – Levy 2004: 59

It has been further explained as:

> In thinking of past and future occurrences, we do so only with reference to a present time. But without a subsistent past and future we could not form any notion of the present. There cannot indeed be a present, since there is neither a past nor a future time. Consciousness alone subsists and consciousness alone is ever present. – Ibid.

The inference may be drawn from the above observations that when time is treated as an object of consciousness, the time and consciousness become inseparable. In this context, it is stated that "now time, or the notion of succession, is one such object: and time too is consciousness objectified" (ibid.: 60).

It may, however, be pointed out that according to Vedānta, time and space are treated as one. This is explained below.

TIME AND SPACE AS ONE

Einstein's theory of relativity has reassured that space and time are one. In this context, it is mentioned:

> Time is not completely separate from independent of space, but is combined with it to form an object called space-time. – Hawking 1988: 23

The following observation also supports the above view that space and time are one:

> Objects in order to exist must endure, that is, duration or time is necessary for the existence of objects, for, without duration there could be nothing to endure. Conversely, the existence of duration depends upon objects, for without objects to endure, there could be no duration; and in this sense, time and objects are one. It follows that space and time are also one. – Wilber 2002: 82

Space and Time as Illusion

Since one cannot perceive empty space, what is perceived as space is the material things located in it. However, the material objects located in space are inseparable from the act of perceiving. In that, the correspondence between the material objects and sense organ is an immediate and inseparable connection. It is the nature of sense organ to manifest sensations. What is cognized by the mind is not the material object but it is due the sensations created by sense organ. But it ought to be recognized that no object located in space has been cognized. This has been interpreted in two ways:

i. sensations caused by stimuli to the senses are illusion (Levy 2004: 32), and

ii. the experience is a mental product.

"That being so, there is at no time a stimulus external to senses" (ibid.: 33). That apart, the fact remains that space exists as an objective reality apart from the mind.

It may be noted that according to science the physical world in which we are living is a mass of atoms, and molecules and vibrations are playing between them. In the context, the following observation solicites attention:

> When the vibrations emanating from these atoms and molecules or the atoms and the molecules themselves strike the sense organs, which are also aggregates of atoms and molecules, sensations are produced. The colours and forms, odors, etc. we perceive do not exist in the atoms and molecules constituting the external objects. They spring up in our mind as a result of the stimulus applied to our sense organs. They exist in our mind and as the mind throws outward the mental image by the process of *vikṣepa* ... we see them outside us and think they exist in the object. This is fundamental illusion of sense perception from which all of us suffer. – Taimni 2005: 342

It may be noted that *vikṣepa* is a mysterious process of mental projection.

TIME

Time is also perceived through events. This is mainly due to the fact that empty time cannot be perceived, as mentioned earlier. Therefore, time itself has no existence, unless we think of it as mentioned above.

It may, however, be stated:

> The essential nature of time is the succession of mental images in our mind. If there is no succession of mental images there would be no time. It is this succession of mental images which produces the impression of change and the mind is led to assume that there must be a duration in which changes take place.
>
> – Taimni 2005: 357-58

This duration is connected with succession of mental images in continuous manner and it is treated as time. But the fact is that this

> passage of time or duration is connected intimately with the succession of mental images in our mind and that the succession of these mental images may be discontinuous like the images projected on a cinema screen without our being aware of the discontinuity. – Ibid.: 360

This has been explained in Patañjali's *Yogasūtra* IV.33:

> The process corresponding to moments which become apprehensible in the final end of transformation (of the *guṇas*) is *kramaḥ*. – Taimni 1999: 439
>
> *Kramaḥ* stands for this process consisting of a relentless succession of discontinuous changes underlying all kinds of phenomena. This process is ultimately based upon the unit of time, *kṣaṇa* as the projection of the cinematographic picture is based upon each opening and closing of aperture. As *kṣaṇa* succeeds *kṣaṇa* the whole manifested world passes from one distinct state to another distinct state, but the succession is so rapid that we are not conscious of the discontinuity. – Ibid.: 441

The above observations indicate that time and space are illusions.

One thing that stands out quite clearly is that concepts like space and time have their existence mainly in the manifestation or appearance of the Absolute Reality which happens to be pure consciousness (*Brahman*) according to Vedānta. In other words, these concepts have only in relative existence.

Philosophy of Bauddha Dharma: Mādhyamika System

SPACE

Space cannot exist as a completely uncharacterized entity. It somehow acquires characteristic (Garfield 1995: 14). This means that everything has characteristic (ibid.: 14, V.2). If this characteristic is examined along with verse XXIV.18 which shows that whatever is dependently co-arisen, it may turn out to be as emptiness (ibid.: 69). Since space exists along with objects, on this account too it is treated as empty entity. Similar is the case with time.

TIME

Time might be thought to exist in relation to things that change. But as changing things (*bhāva*) have been shown to be untenable, the reality of Time too is not established (Murti 2003: 199-200). Further, the existence of time apart from things becomes an empty one. The empty time cannot be perceived. Therefore, time itself has no existence.

YOGĀCĀRA VIJÑĀNAVĀDA BUDDHISM

Space and time are one in the sense that both are manifestations of consciousness (Hanh 2008: 179). However, it is stated:

> We usually think of space as something empty. But physicists have shown that when matter is diluted, it becomes space. The theory of relativity shows that space and matter are one reality. If, there is no space; there is no matter. If there is no matter, there is no space. Space – a seemingly empty phenomenon – is able to bend matter, a seemingly solid phenomenon. – Ibid.: 179-80

It is further stated:

> Time makes space, and space makes time. Outside of time, there can be no space. Outside of space, there can be no time. Einstein has said clearly that space and time are two aspects of the same reality.
>
> – Hanh 2008: 180

However, Time and space inter-are. We cannot separate one from the other. Both are manifestations of consciousness (Ibid.). Therefore, it may be said that time and space have no independent existence apart from self-consciousness.

Time and Space (Eternity and Infinity)

In the context of time, the following observations are worth of consideration:

> Past and future collapse into now, before and after collapse into present, linearity collapses into simultaneity, and time vanishes into Eternity. ... This present moment contains all time and is therefore itself timeless, and hence *this timeless present is Eternity itself* – a moment without date or duration, extension or succession, past or future, before or after, having the whole of its existence simultaneously, which is the nature of Eternity.
>
> – Wilber 2002: 86

What is infinity to space is explained below:

> Now Eternity is to time, what Infinity is to space. That is, just as all of Infinity is completely present at every point of space, so also all of eternity is completely present at every point of time. Thus, from the viewpoint of Eternity, absolutely all time is *NOW*, just as to the infinity, all space is HERE. Since all time is NOW, it follows that the past and the future are much illusions, and that only Reality is present Reality.
>
> – Ibid.: 79

These observations are, however, supported by scientists.

> There is no past and future. There is eternality, the *now*. There is no "there". It is *here* only. This concept was given by Hermann

> Minkowski who was Einstein's mathematics teacher. He was very much inspired by his student's special theory of relativity. He deduced a space–time diagram out of his mathematical explorations. In this diagram, the past, the present and the future are mathematically related. All the past and all the future for each individual meet, and ever meet, at one single point of *now* in the diagram. The *now* of each individual is specifically located *here* (wherever the observer is) and nowhere else. Minkowski's diagram has got much philosophical significance. In the relative world where knowledge is variable depending upon the states of the observers, there can also be the invariant concept *now* and *here*.
>
> – Panda 2008: 66

Hume's Philosophy (Time and Space)

SPACE

It seems that David Hume has not made any attempt to distinguish between different patterns of change, which may be derived from the experience. Further, Hume has not defined space directly, but it can be inferred from the following observations:

> The table before me alone is sufficient by its view to give me the idea of extension. This idea is then borrowed from, and represents some impression, which this moment appears to the senses. But my senses convey to me only the impressions of *coloured points* disposed in a certain manner. If the eye is sensible of any thing farther, I desire it may be pointed out to me. But if it be impossible to show any thing farther, we may conclude with certainty that the idea of extension is nothing but a copy of these *coloured points and the manner of their appearance.*
>
> – Hume 1951: 41

The concept of space has been further explained by the fact that

> if the idea of extension really can exist, as we were conscious, it does, its parts must also exist; and in order to that, must be considered as coloured or tangible. We have, therefore, no idea of space or extension, but when we regard it as an object either of our sight or feeling.
>
> – Ibid.: 45

It is, thus, evident that according to Hume, the space can be conceived only when it is regarded as an object either by our sight or by our feeling.

TIME

Hume's conception of time is explained in the following observations. He has examined time through events.

> All this reasoning takes place with regard to time; along with an additional argument, which it may be proper to take notice of. It is a property inseparable from time, and which in a manner constitutes its essence, that each of its parts succeeds another, and that none of them, however contiguous, can ever be coexistent. For the same reason, that the year 1737 cannot concur with the present year 1738, every moment must be distinct from, and posterior or antecedent to another. It is certain then, that time, as it exists, must be composed of indivisible moments. For if in time we could never arrive at an end of division, and if each moment, as it succeeds another, were not perfectly single and indivisible, there would be an infinite number of coexistent moments, or parts of time; which I believe will be allowed to be an arrant contradiction. – Hume 1951: 38

Time can also be perceived when "the indivisible moments of time must be filled with some real object or existence, whose succession forms the duration, and makes it be conceivable by the mind" (ibid.: 45).

Kant's Philosophy

Space and time have been defined by Immanuel Kant as follows:

> *Space*: Space is nothing else than the form of all phenomena of the external sense, that is, the subjective condition of the sensibility, under which alone external intuition is possible.
> – Meiklejohn 2010-13: 47

> *Time*: Time is nothing else than the form of the internal sense, that is, of the intuitions of self and of our internal state. For time

> cannot be any determination of outward phenomena. It has to do neither with shape nor position; on the contrary, it determines the relation of representations in our internal state.
>
> – Meiklejohn 2010-13: 51

It is thus evident that space and time are explained by Kant through intuition and representation. In this context, the following observation is worth stating:

> All our intuition is nothing but the representation of phenomena; that the things which, we intuite, are not in themselves the same as our representations of them in intuition, nor are their relations in themselves so constituted as they appear to us; and that if we take away the subject, or even only the subjective constitution of our senses in general, then not only the nature and relations of objects in space and time, but even space and time themselves disappear; and these as phenomena cannot exist in themselves, but only in us. – Ibid.: 56

The above definitions and explanations may be summed up as follows: Space is perceived by outer sense and time is the form of inner sense. Both (space and time) cannot exist in themselves but that exist in us (human beings have representations of space–time). This is fairly comparable to Vedāntic conception of space and time. The latter is viewed by conscious human being subjectively as time and the former is perceived objectively as space. This has already been mentioned earlier in this chapter.

The other observation on Kant is: "Space and time are empirically real, but transcendently ideal" (Chatterjea et al. 2014: 78). This means that space and time have only relative existence. This view is also quite similar to Vedānta, in which space and time have only relative existence as mentioned earlier.

METAPHYSICAL EXPOSITION OF SPACE AND TIME

Space is not a conception, but it is an intuition, derived from outward experiences (Meiklejohn 2010-13: 45). In this context, it is stated that "Kant just tells us what outer sense does" (Chatterjea et al. 2014: 58). However, the inner sense, perceives time as the form.

> In inner sense we are perceiving our own mental representations, which are our own thoughts, beliefs, sensations: whatever is happening within us. – Ibid.

But "inner sense does not give any knowledge of oneself as one is" (ibid.: 58-59). That apart, the fact remains that

> both in inner sense and in outer sense, what is given are appearances. We neither know the things in themselves nor can we know our own soul. – Ibid.: 59

Now what are space and time? It has already been stated that space is perceived by outer sense and time is the form which is perceived by inner sense.

> So all our inner experiences we perceive as ordered in time, they come one after another and all that we perceive by outer sense is in space, outside of us. So here is the thesis, *space is the form of outer sense and time is the form of inner sense.* – Ibid.

According to Kant, time is experienced at two levels: original and derived. The original time experience is the form of inner sense. Whereas, "the derived time is also experienced as a form in which things happen in space" (ibid.). It may be noted that time happens to be the forms of both senses, indicating thereby time gets a priority over space. This is because,

> space has a limited role, but time encompasses space within itself because even the things that we perceive in space are also in time. – Ibid.: 59-60

However, imagination is the faculty dealing with time. In this context, the following observation is made:

> In imagination, we remember the past which is gone and anticipate the future, which is not yet. The function of imagination is always to keep the time which is escaping us under our grip. Without

> imagination, we cannot know anything. A process which is caught up in the flow of time requires imagination to still have a control of it. If we were being which is not caught up in time that is to say whose experiences are not ordered in time we would not need imagination. – Chatterjea et al. 2014: 60

According to Kant, space is a necessary representation a priori,

> which serves for all the foundation of all external intuitions. We never can imagine or make a representation to ourselves of the non-existence of space, though we may easily enough think that no objects are found in it. – Meiklejohn 2010-13: 45-46

It is representation a priori, providing the basis of external phenomena.

Similarly, time is also

> a necessary representation, laying at the foundation of all our intuitions. With regard to phenomena in general, we cannot think away time from them, and represent them to ourselves as out of and unconnected with time, but we can quite well represent to ourselves time void of phenomena. Time is, therefore, given a priori. In it alone is all reality of phenomena possible. – Ibid.: 49

Kant's third argument is that "space is one that there are not many spaces, which are not parts of one space" (Chatterjea et al. 2014: 67). However, multiplicity in it depends solely upon the limitations. Space is based on the principle of geometry having, "in a triangle, two sides together are greater than one third" (Meiklejohn 2010-13: 46). This shows that space has three dimensions. Whereas, "time has only one dimension. Different times are not coexistent but successive" (ibid.: 50). Further, time is an irreversible, one-dimensional flow. This is explained as follows:

> The idea that time's flow is irreversible and my consciousness always is at a moment (point) that is always a now. I am always in a now. The past is gone on this picture. But then how do I hope the sense of the past? For, I would be confined in the solipsism of the now. How does the past at all arise in me? One might

> say by memory. That is a true answer. But on this picture, the memory is not there, the memory is again in another now. This means the fact of remembering does not help to escape from the solipsism of the now. So one can never get rid of this now and have a conception of the past and the future.
>
> – Chatterjea et al. 2014: 74-75

Kant's fourth argument is that "space is represented as *infinite given magnitude*" (ibid.: 68). In this context, it is stated:

> People found it peculiar that space would be both given and infinite or that it is given as an infinite magnitude. We might say space is not given as infinite magnitude, we only see the finite spaces, i.e. to say space, which is bound by a horizon. Kant's point, I think, was that since there is only one space, different spaces are limitations of the one space. – Ibid.: 68-69

In the case of time also it is pointed out that

> the infinity of time signifies nothing more than that every determined quantity of time is possible through the limitations of one time lying at the foundation. – Meiklejohn 2010-13: 50

PRIORITY OF TIME OVER SPACE

So far we have discussed, time and space as one. Even,

> the inner sense and the outer sense go together with regard to their certainty. They are on the same level. Both are equally certain. Even then, one must concede that for Kant inner sense has priority. But that was not with regard to certainty. There is a priority because space is the form only of outer sense and time is the form of both outer and inner. – Chatterjea et al. 2014: 87

In this context, it is quite important to know how one experiences time. This is explained below:

> I experience myself in time, and time is the form of my internal self-experience. No experience of myself is of reality, but only of appearances. I appear to myself, I do not know myself really as I am, any more than I know how really things are. In both cases,

> through inner sense I only intuit appearances. As an appearance, I am in time although as a thing in itself, I am not in time. I do not know myself. Kant held, "Time is in me and I am in time". The container is at the same time the contained. I contain time, but time also contains me. This shows that I can think of myself indifferent ways. I can think of everything in two different ways: as appearance and as the thing in itself. When I think of myself as appearance then I am in time, but if think of myself as I am in reality then I am not in time, time is rather the form of my sensibility. – Chatterjea et al. 2014: 85-86

Scientific Views on Space and Time

According to Einstein's General Theory of Relativity, (i) space is relative, and (ii) time is also relative.

> Time is not an independent entity separate from space; there is no such thing as space and time; there is only space–time.
> – Panda 2008: 59

Both are connected and there is a four-dimensional continuum called space–time continuum.

The theory of relativity has, however, revolutionized the concept of space and time and put an end to the idea of absolute time which is advocated by both Aristotle and Newton (Hawking 1988: 18). According to the theory of relativity,

> each observer must have his own measure of time, as recorded by a clock carried with him, and that identical clocks carried by different observers would not necessarily agree. – Ibid.: 21

It is observed that

> in the general theory of relativity, the framework of the special theory is extended to include gravity. The effect of gravity, according to general theory, is to make space–time curved.
> – Capra 1989: 191

The curvature of space is caused by the gravitational fields of massive bodies (ibid.: 194).

It is further stated:

> Since space can never be separated from time in relativity theory, the curvature caused by gravity cannot be limited to three-dimensional space, but must extend to four-dimensional space–time and this is, indeed, what the general theory of relativity theory predicts. – Capra 1989: 194-95

In this context, one would say:

> In a curved space–time, the distortions caused by the curvature affect not only the spatial relationships described by geometry but also the lengths of time intervals. Time does not flow at the same rate as in the flat space–time, and as the curvature varies from place to place, according to the distribution of massive bodies, so does the flow of time. It is important to realize, however, that this variation of the flow of time can only be seen by an observer who remains in a different place from the clocks used to measure the variation. – Ibid.: 195

However, it is observed that one can have better comprehension of space through the concept of field introduced by Michael Faraday and James Clark Maxwell in the nineteenth century.

> The quantum field is seen as the fundamental physical entity; a continuous medium which is present everywhere in space. Particles are merely local condensations of the field: concentrations of energy which come and go, thereby losing their individual character and dissolving into the underlying field.
> – Ibid.: 233

It may be noted that "the field is the only reality" (ibid.).

Yet, there is confusion among some scientists about the nature of space and field.

> They think that space is the container and field is the content. In their view, space is permeated with field. ... This is, however, not correct. As a matter of fact, space is itself field. – Panda 2008: 313

In this context, the following observations are important for establishing the similarity between science and Indian philosophy: Vedānta and Vijñānavāda Buddhism.

> Whatever may be the controversy regarding "field in space" or "field as space", science has discarded the concept of pluralism and has accepted field or space as one and a single continuous entity as the basis of appearance of multifarious world. This basic entity is one and continuous; it is the source of the heterogeneous manifestation of the universe. The one gives rise to many; the invisible gives rise to multifarious invisible-cum-visible ones; the formless gives rise to pluralities of forms. Thus monism is established in science. At the field or space level, the world is monistic. At the level of the corpuscles, the world is pluralistic. In spite of this apparent pluralism, the micro particles communicate among themselves, although they may be far apart at billions of light-years away and this communication too occurs without any time-interval. Scientists have been very puzzled to explain this phenomenon. – Panda 2008: 313

The monism of science may, however, be supported by both Advaita Vedānta and Yogācāra Vijñānavāda Buddhism. This is mainly due to the fact that both have accepted only consciousness as the reality. Vedānta has treated the empirical world as relative existence, which happens to be quite illusory. Whereas, Vijñānavāda Buddhism has categorically rejected the existence of external world. The above concept of one and many is also supported by Vedānta, because pure consciousness is one; when manifests through mind it becomes many. The teaching of the *Avataṁsakasūtra* of Vijñānavāda Buddhism says that "one is in the all and the all is in the one", suggesting thereby the concept of one and many (Misra 2014: 50), as mentioned in the above observation.

Consciousness and Time

According to Aristotle, "it is impossible that time should exist if consciousness did not" (Balslev 1999: 136). This in a way indicates that the existence of time depends upon the existence of consciousness. It is in conformity with Vedānta, in which time is treated as the object of consciousness. However, according to Krishnamurti, "consciousness is the result of time" (1992: 71). Time being an "arrow" moving onwards, it does not know in itself. In fact, it is the consciousness which makes the time into past, present and future. It also ought to be recognized that when consciousness descends in human being, it manifests through mind. In that, it becomes self-consciousness, which knows not only external world, but also knows itself. It may be noted that there is no other entity in the entire universe, which knows itself except self-consciousness existing in human beings. In such a situation, it is difficult to understand how the time can create consciousness as mentioned in the discourses of Krishnamurti. We are presenting here the views of Sartre on consciousness and time because it contains both the views: Vedānta and Krishnamurti. This is evident from the following statement:

> Consciousness is the source of time and time, in turn, transforms consciousness to a temporal consciousness for time is the very propulsive heart of consciousness. – Thomas 2004: 127

TEMPORALITY OF CONSCIOUSNESS

According to Sartre, consciousness introduces temporality not only in time but also into other things. This is "precisely because, consciousness is temporal" (Sartre 1984: 29). This shows that

> temporality is a dimension of human consciousness. He thinks that the being of human reality is itself time. – Bhadra 2004: 362

Sartre (1984: 807) has defined temporality as:

> Subjective process whereby the for-itself continuously lives its project of nihilating the in-itself. Through temporality the for-itself sets up its own measure for the duration and self-identity of things. Time is not in things but flows over them. The for-itself as what it has been (Past), is a flight (Present) toward what it projects to be (Future).

It has been further explained:

> The for-itself endures in the form of a non-thetic consciousness (of) enduring. But I can feel the time which flows; and apprehend myself as a unity of succession. In this case I am conscious of enduring. This consciousness is thetic and resembles a knowledge just as duration which is temporalized under my regard is roughly like an object of knowledge. – Sartre 1984: 211

What is the relationship between non-thetic consciousness and thetic consciousness is explained below.

NON-THETIC AND THETIC CONSCIOUSNESS

The non-thetic consciousness is also known as non-positional or pre-reflective consciousness. Whereas thetic consciousness is positional or reflective consciousness. These are explained below:

> I have just read a story, and I recall my reading in seeking to account for my experience. There was pre-reflective consciousness of the book, of the heroes of the novel; furthermore, there was an inner awareness of consciousness of all this. This inner awareness of consciousness is called "non-positional consciousness of itself", i.e. self-consciousness. Neither consciousness of objects nor self-consciousness was anyway experienced as related to the ego.
>
> – Medhidhammaporn 1995: 25

This shows that the ego does not appear in the pre-reflective consciousness. So is the case with Vedānta; there is no ego in pure consciousness.

In the Sartrean framework, the ego appears only in the reflective consciousness (ibid.: 31). Therefore, it may be said that the pre-reflective consciousness is egoless, and it is the non-positional self-consciousness. Whereas, the reflective consciousness has the ego and in that it becomes the positional consciousness. This is explained in the following quotation:

> All consciousness is positional in that it transcends itself in order to reach an object, and it exhausts itself in this same

> positing. All that there is of *intention* in my actual consciousness is directed toward the outside, toward the table; all my judgements or practical activities, all my present inclinations transcend themselves; they aim at the table and are absorbed in it. ... However, the necessary and sufficient condition for a knowing consciousness to be knowledge of its objects is that it be consciousness of itself as being that knowledge. – Sartre 1984: 11

The reflective consciousness cannot be separated from the pre-reflective consciousness. This is evident from the fact that "every positional consciousness of an object is at the same time a non-positional consciousness itself" (ibid.: 13).

In this context, it has been further clarified that

> reflection has no kind of primacy over the consciousness reflected-on. It is not reflection which reveals the consciousness reflected-on to itself. Quite the contrary, it is the non-reflective consciousness which renders the reflection possible; there is pre-reflective cogito which is the condition of the Cartesian cogito.
> – Ibid.

It emerges that without pre-reflective (non-thetic, non-positional) consciousness, the reflective (thetic-positional) consciousness is not possible. In such a situation,

> it is agreed then that reflection must be united to that which is reflected-on by a bond of being that the reflective consciousness must be the consciousness reflected-on. – Ibid.: 213

This reflected-on is pre-reflective (non-thetic, non-positional) consciousness. However, "the reflected-on, itself, is its past and its future" (ibid.: 219).

It may be noted that

> the reflected-on is profoundly altered by reflection in this sense that it is self-consciousness as the consciousness reflected-on of this or that transcendent phenomenon. The reflected-on knows itself observed. – Ibid.: 214

That apart, the pre-reflective consciousness being temporal, is an "ekstatic unity", which simultaneously exists in three dimensions of past, present and future (Medhidhammaporn 1995: 55).

How these three dimensions are related to one another to form their unity is stated below.

THE PAST

If the temporal phenomenon is considered in its totality, it would be possible to see:

> My past is first of all *mine*; that is, that it exists as function of a certain being which I am. The past is not nothing; neither is it the present; but at its very source, it is bound to a certain present and to a certain future to both of which it belongs. ... It is originally the past of this present. – Sartre 1984: 163

However, the past consciousness is not separated from the present consciousness. This is evident from the fact that

> the prior consciousness is always *there* (though with the modification of pastness). It constantly maintains a relation of interpretation with the present consciousness, but on the basis of this existential relation it is put out of the game, out of the circuit, between parentheses. – Ibid.: 64

It is clearly stated:

> For Human reality alone the existence of a past is manifest because it has been established that human reality *has to be what it is*. It is through the for-itself that the past arrives in the world because its "I am" is in the form of an *I am me.* – Ibid.: 168

However, the for-itself is such that

> it has the right to turn back on itself toward its own origin. The being by which the "Why" comes into being has the right to posit its own "Why" since it is itself an interrogation, a "Why". – Ibid.: 788

The existence of past has been reassured by Sartre. This is evident from the following:

> Death reunites us with ourselves. Eternity has changed us into ourselves. At the moment of death we are: that is, we are defenceless before the judgements of others. They can decide in *truth* what we are: ultimately we have no longer any chance of escape from what an all knowing intelligence could do. ... By death the for-itself is changed forever into an in-itself in that it has slipped entirely into the past. Thus, the past is the ever-growing totality of the in-itself which we are. – Sartre 1984: 169

Being in-itself is non-conscious Being. "It is the Being of the phenomenon and overflows the knowledge which we have of it. It is plenitude, and strictly speaking we can say of it only that it is" (ibid.: 800).

Sartre says that "My essence is in the past" (ibid.: 175). However, "existence precedes essence" (ibid.: 725).

THE PRESENT

The in-itself is the past. As against this, the present happens to be the for-itself, which is defined here as presence to being (ibid.: 177). From the for-itself,

> the present enters into the world; the beings of the world are co-present, in fact, just insofar as one and the same for itself is at the same time present to all of them. – Ibid.

It is further stated that

> the for-itself is a witness of itself in the presence of being as not being that being; presence to being is the presence of the for-itself insofar as the for-itself is not. – Ibid.: 178

In fact,

> The present is precisely this negation of being, this escape from being inasmuch as being is *there* as that from which one escapes. The For-itself is present to being in the form of flight: the Present

> is a perpetual flight in the face of being. Thus, we have precisely defined the fundamental meaning of the Present: the Present is *not*. – Sartre 1984: 179

It may, however, be noted that

> at present it is not what it is (past) and it is what it is not (future). Here then we are referred to the future. – Ibid.

THE FUTURE

The future arrives in the world only through human reality.

> The future, like the past, does not exist as a phenomenon of that original temporality of being-in-itself. – Ibid.: 180

However, the future in terms of consciousness has described in the following observation:

> The For-itself is the thetic consciousness of the world in the form of presence and non-thetic self-consciousness. Thus, what is ordinarily revealed to consciousness is the *future world* without consciousness being aware that it is the world insofar as it will appear to a consciousness, the world insofar as it is posited as future by the presence of a For-itself to come. This world has meaning as future only insofar as I am present to it as *another* who I *will be*, in another position, physical, emotional, social, etc. Yet it is this which is at the end of my present For-itself and beyond being-in-itself, and this is the reason why we have a tendency first to present the future as a state of the world and to make it appear subsequently on the ground of the world. – Ibid.: 183-84

It may be noted:

> The future is the ideal point where the sudden infinite comprehension of facticity (past) of the For-itself (present), and of its possible (a particular Future) will at last cause the *Self* to arise as the existence in-itself of the For-itself. The project of the For-itself toward the future which it is a project toward the in-itself. – Ibid.: 184-85

However, "the future constitutes the meaning of my present For-itself, as the project of its possibility" (Sartre 1984: 185).

THE ECSTATIC UNITY OF CONSCIOUSNESS

It is stated that "it is impossible to conceive of a consciousness which would not exist in these three dimensions" (ibid.: 196). In that, three requirements are to be fulfilled. These are:

i. to not be what it is,
ii. to be what it is not, and
iii. to be what it is not and to not be what it is.

These three requirements are within the unity of a perpetual referring. "Here we are dealing with three ecstatic dimensions: the meaning of the ecstases is distance from self" (ibid.). In this context, it may be stated that, "consciousness (in the present) is not what it is (past), it is what it is not (the future)" (Thomas 2004: 127).

It may be noted that "not what is" is used in the sense of past. Whereas, it is what it is not is a possibility for future. Consciousness is treated as nothingness by Sartre mainly because everything exists outside of consciousness. In this context, it is observed that "consciousness can exist simultaneously in the three ecstases of past, present and future because at the present it is nothingness" (Medhidhammaporn 1995: 61).

3

Thought as the Source of Nature and Quantum Physics

Introduction

THIS chapter attempts to discuss two main issues:

i. thought as the source of nature (Mukerji 1957: 214), and

ii. modern physics' tendency to undermine the principle of causation (ibid.: 224).

In the quantum theory, causality has been replaced by what is called the principle of indeterminacy (ibid.: 225).

Thought as the source of nature does not seem to be appropriate in the sense that it becomes the object of self-consciousness, which is embodied in human being known as *jīvātman* (self) according to the Advaita Vedānta school of Indian philosophy. An inference may, therefore, be drawn that it is the self-consciousness rather than thought, which becomes the source of nature. It may be mentioned here that self-consciousness while knowing the objective world, it knows itself. There is no other entity which knows itself.

However, the main feature of the implicate order of quantum physics is that it has extended to the field of consciousness, so as "to comprehend both cosmos and consciousness as a single-unbroken totality of movement" (Bohm 2012: 219). The implicate order in a way to represent ourselves, as the order present to the senses. This is stated below:

> The fact that this order is actually more or less the one appearing to our senses. ... This can be done only when we bring consciousness into our universe of discourse and show that

> matter in general and consciousness in particular, at least in a certain sense, have this implicate (manifest) order in common.
> – Bohm 2012: 236

It also ought to be recognized that matter itself is causality, which is explained as:

> For matter is absolutely nothing but causality. ... Its being is its acting; it is not possible to conceive for it any other being. Only as something acting does it fill space and time; its action on the immediate object (which is itself matter) conditions the perception in which alone it exists. The consequence of the action of every material object on another is known only insofar as the latter now acts on the immediate object in a way different from that in which it acted previously; it consists in this alone. Thus cause and effect are the whole essence and nature of matter. ... Its whole being and essence consist only in the orderly and regular change produced by one part of it in another; consequently, its being and essence are entirely relative.
> – Cross 2014: 63

The Quantum Theory of Physics

It is observed:

> The quantum theory is, at present, the most basic way available in physics for understanding the fundamental and universal laws relating to matter and its movement. – Bohm 2012: xv

The universe is regarded as a continuous field, but according to the quantum theory, the field is discontinuous. This is equally applicable to

> particle-like, and that it is as undermined in its actual behaviour as is required in the particle view of relation as whole. – Ibid.: xv

According to the quantum theory, the

> movement is in general discontinuous in the sense that action is constituted of *indivisible quanta* (implying also that an electron,

> for example, can go from one state to another, without passing through any states in between). – Bohm 2012: 222

However, the electron is never separated from a certain quantum field which fundamentally affects it and exhibits certain novel features.

> This quantum field satisfies Schrodinger's equation, just as the electromagnetic field satisfies Maxell's equation. It, too, is therefore causality determined. – Bohm and Peat 1987: 88

In the causal interpretation, "the electron moves under own energy but the formation is the *form* of the quantum wave directs the energy of electron" (ibid.: 90). This is further, explained below:

i. The electron travels towards a screen containing two slits. Clearly, it can go through only one slit on the other. But the quantum wave can pass through both. On the outgoing side of the slit system, the quantum waves interfere to provide a highly complex quantum potential which does not generally fall off with the distance from the slits. ... In the deep valleys and broad plateaus, the quantum potential changes rapidly. In these regions, there is a strong force on the particle which is deflected, even though there is no classical fares operating. The movement of the electron is, therefore, modified to produce the scattering pattern. In this case the wave-like properties do not arise in any essential duality of the quantum particle but from the complex effects of the potential (ibid.: 90-93).
ii. The explanation of the quantum properties of the electron given above emphasized how the *form* of the quantum potential can dominate behaviour. In other words, information contained within quantum potential will determine the outcome of a quantum process (ibid.: 93).
iii. Consider a radio wave, whose form carries a signal – the voice of an announcer, for example. The energy of the sound that is heard from the radio does not, in fact, come from

this wave but from the batteries or power plug. This latter energy is essentially "unformed", but take up its form from the information within the radio wave. This information is *potentially* active everywhere but only *actually* active when its form enters into the electrical energy of the radio (Bohm and Peat 1987: 93).

iv. The analogy with the causal interpretation is clear. The quantum wave carries "information" and is, therefore, *potentially* active everywhere, but it is *actually* active only when and where this energy enters into the energy of the particle. But this implies that an electron, or any other elementary particle, has a complex and subtle inner structure that is at least comparable with that of a radio. Clearly, this notion goes against the whole tradition of modern physics, which assumes that as matter is analysed into smaller and smaller parts, its behaviour grows more elementary. By contrast, the casual interpretation suggests that nature may be more subtle and strange than was previously thought (ibid.).

In quantum theory, however, it is not possible to speak of the particle's trajectory

> when we say that the particle is also wave. What we mean is that the wave pattern as a whole is a manifestation of the particle. The picture of travelling waves is thus totally different from that of travelling particles. – Capra 1989: 165

It may further be stated that in quantum theory the atomic phenomena can be described in terms of probabilities. Therefore, it can never be said that atomic particle exists at a certain place nor can it be said that it does not exist.

> Being a probability pattern, the particle has tendencies to exist in various places and thus manifests a strange kind of physical reality between existence and non-existence. We cannot,

> therefore, describe the state of the particle in terms of fixed opposite concepts.
> – Capra 1989: 166

The duality of the particle has been resolved through the probability waves in the sense that the pair of opposites is transcended by the atomic reality (ibid.). Yet, it is most difficult to accept this transcendental theory of quantum physics (ibid.: 167). This duality has, however, been reconciled in another way. It is stated:

> A photon, or an electron, has a dual aspect, a wave aspect and a particle aspect. Two aspects are complementary. The one aspect excludes the other aspect. That is why the two aspects are not contradictory. A contradiction between them could arise only if the two aspects could be observed at the same time. But this never happens; and we have compelling theoretical arguments that this could not happen. *The wave and the particle aspects are complementary and not contradictory* (emphasis added by italics).
> – Kothari 2002: 311

It has been further explained:

> At the root of the wave-particle duality is the principle of absolute indistinguishability, absolute identity of particles of the same kind. All electrons in the universe are absolutely identical, absolutely indistinguishable from one another. – Ibid.: 313

In the total wave function, the identity of individual electron is completely lost. There is no separate individuality of electron in the total wave function. This is explained below.

The Concept of One in Many and Many in One

> *The electrons have submerged themselves, as it were in one "brotherhood" of electrons.* The Many have become One ... when we speak of the total-wave-function or the field, and the many identical particles incorporated in the wave function. It is not sort of an aggregate, a sum of the Many. In an aggregate, the Oneness is no more than an euphemism for the Many that are still visible, may be dimly in the aggregate. The concept of Oneness

> in quantum mechanics is a totally, fundamentally, new concept. It has no analogy, no parallel, whatever in classical physics or in everyday experience. Common sense fails to be of any aid. The One is an abstract space, the Many in physical space. The two aspects are complementary (emphasis added by italics).
>
> – Kothari 2002: 314

The above concept of One in Many and Many in One in the case of electron may be supported by the *Avataṁsakasūtra* of Vijñānavāda school of Buddhist philosophy. Although the Sūtra has not been incorporated in the teaching of Vijñānavāda (Hanh 2008: 81), its teachings of interbeing and interpenetration are very important for unlocking the door of reality and get rid of our notions concerning the world (ibid.: 83). The main teaching of the *Avataṁsakasūtra* is stated as follows:

> *The one is in the all, and the all is in the one.* One thing contains everything else. In the everything is the one. In our own age, atomic physicists who have looked deeply into the molecular world have had to abandon concepts of inside and outside, self and other. They know that one atom is made up of all other atoms. One electron is made up of all other electrons. In a molecule or an atom, we can see the presence of all other molecules and atoms. One atom contains the whole universe. *In one person everything in the universe is present* (emphasis added by italics). – Ibid.: 162-63

The *Bṛhadāraṇyaka Upaniṣad* too supports the concept of One in Many and Many in One. It says:

> Being an organic product of *Ātman*, everything in the world has got essentially to be of the same nature as *Ātman* with its dual capacity of forming the centre and the periphery of the everything. – Singh 2004: 254

This is illustrated by means of fifteen examples taken from physical elements, luminaries and certain human values, organizations and creations (ibid.).

> *Ātman* is the controller of all both from inside and outside as are

> the centre and periphery of the wheel serving as the controller of the spokes. – Singh 2004: 255

The example of earth is described as follows:

> *As the essence of all and all as the essence of the earth.* This fantastic relativity of things happens to be visualized by the sage particularly in view of the earth and every product of it having envisioned as an abode of one and the same *Ātman*. It is interesting here to note the point of difference in the concept of relativity as mooted out by the Upaniṣad in this instance and as formulated by Albert Einstein. While Einstein's theory of relativity makes out the relativity of things with reference to spatio-temporal measurements, the Upaniṣadic sage goes back to the *Ātman* as the root of everything including time and space. In his view, the earth's capacity to form the essence of everything born on this earth as well as the capacity of everything born on this earth to form the essence of the earth, arises from the fact that the earth as well as each one of its products has got embodied in it one and the same *Ātman* (emphasis added by italics). – Ibid.: 254

Similar type of explanation has been given for the other examples such as water, air, sun and moon, as mentioned above.

According to Advaita Vedānta, the self is *caitanya* (consciousness) itself and it shines in its own light: it is called *svayam-prakāśa* (self-shining). This consciousness is not a contingent product of an interaction between the subject and the object (Datta 1998: 42). One can, however, experience self-shining or pure consciousness in dreamless sleep in which the dualism of the "I" and "not I" (*aham* and *idam*) vanishes altogether (ibid.: 44). But it would not be correct to state that in such a state, consciousness ceases to be, because the consciousness according to Vedānta is permanent and eternal (Thibaut 1994: 121). Further, in dreamless sleep, one experiences that "I have slept well", indicating thereby the actual existence of some pleasant experience – a blissful consciousness (Datta 1998: 44).

This dreamless consciousness is interpreted as *nirvikalpaka jñāna*. When this consciousness gets differentiated, it becomes *savikalpaka jñāna* (ibid.). It is thus evident that *one* undifferentiated consciousness (i.e. pure consciousness in dreamless sleep) becomes *Many* as differentiating consciousness (i.e. *savikalpaka jñāna*) in manifestation.

It may be stated that One in Many and Many in One are possible

> because the self is consciousness. Consciousness can assume many forms without endangering its non-duality. Even while being aware of the many, consciousness itself does not cease to be one. Everything is rooted in consciousness. And even after the myriad possible objects are eliminated, consciousness will still remain.
> – Grimes 1992: 107-08

It is important to recognize that in quantum physics, consciousness has a significant role which has no counterpart in classical physics (Kothari 2002: 315). In this context, it is stated:

> To understand the implicate order, Bohm has found it necessary to regard consciousness as an essential feature of the holomovement and to take it accounted explicitly in his theory. – Capra 1989: 353

Matter: Wholeness and Implicate Order

Bohm's contribution in developing a new theory of the relation between consciousness and matter in a scientific manner is the most exciting (ibid.: 352). However, it has been observed:

> In a discussion of the "wave function of the universe", the implicate and generative order of the whole is involved. Out of this whole emerge sub-wholes (including observers), which themselves can be organized into wider contexts, and these in turn are further organized until the total universe is encompassed in this way.
> – Bohm and Peat 1987: 196

An attempt has recently been made to examine the Bohm's contribution in establishing the relationship between consciousness and matter in a logical framework. This is evident from the following observation:

> Matter as a whole can be understood in terms of the notion that the implicate order is the immediate and primary actuality (while the explicate order can be derived as a particular, distinguished case of the implicate order). ... If matter and consciousness could in this way be understood together, in terms of the same general notion of order, the way would be opened to comprehending their relationship on the basis of some common ground. Thus, we could come to the germ of a new notion of unbroken wholeness, in which consciousness is no longer to be fundamentally separated from the matter. David Bohm points out that if all actions are in the form of discreet quanta, the interactions between entities (e.g. electrons) constitute a single structure of indivisible links, so that the entire universe has to be thought of as an unbroken whole. ... Eventually, Bohm points out that matter and consciousness are manifestations of "implicate order", which enfolds all that which is. We may remark that this is strikingly similar to the Vedāntic notion, in the light of which a contradiction between mind and body is resolved. – Joshi 2006: 25-26

What Is Order?

Order has been defined by Bohm in a very broad sense. "Whatever we do presupposes some kind of order" (Bohm and Peat 1987: 111). However, order may be experienced in a number of different ways. For instance,

> there is the order of number, of points on a line, of space and time, of the movement of a particle through space, and of the functioning of a machine. But order need not be only mechanical or restricted to inanimate systems. – Ibid.

Notions of order depend upon one's ability to perceive similarities and differences in reflections. In fact, the perception begins through the gathering of differences and similarities of the object. For instance, in the case of vision, we gather first,

> differences as primary data of vision, which are then used to build of similarities. The order of vision proceeds through the

> perception of differences and the creation of similarities of these differences. – Bohm and Peat 1987: 112

Similar is the case with the thought process, when we think about some objects, some broad images regarding those objects are formed and then categories are formed through a mental perception of their differences from some general background.

It may be stated:

> Order is neither subjective nor objective, for when a new context is revealed, then a different notion of order will appear. – Ibid.: 125

The concept of order is, however, by itself quite general.

> But one of its most fundamental and deepest meanings is that it lies at the root of structure, which is a key issue, not only in science but in life as whole. – Ibid.: 141

Quantum Field Theory and Implicate Order

In the quantum field theory, the implicate order and the causal interpretation are quite simple. It is stated:

> Instead of taking a particle as the fundamental reality, start with the field. ... The field is continuous and by itself would spread out from any source. However, because the super-quantum potential is non-linear and non-local, it is able under certain conditions, to provide a subtle kind of immediate connection between distant regions of the field. – Ibid.: 182

In the causal interpretation of field theory, there are two implicate orders in a specified relationship (ibid.). The first implicate order is the field itself. The second implicate order is explained as follows:

> The second implicate order is then obtained by considering the super-quantum wave function. This is related to the whole field as the original quantum wave function is related to the particle. A more detailed treatment shows that the super-quantum wave function also moves in kind of implicate order

> which is, however, far subtler and more complex than is the first implicate order. This then comprises the second implicate order.
> – Bohm and Peat 1987: 182-83

Implicate Order and Generative Order

The relationship between the implicate order and the generative order is very close. The former is the particular case of the latter. However, the implicate forms are generated in an order of unfoldment. In this process, the whole happens to be quite relevant to each part (ibid.: 184).

> If there are higher implicate orders, then a similar generative order will prevail throughout all the levels. Ultimately, it is, of course, the holomovement and what may lie beyond, from which all is generated. – Ibid.

The implicate order and the explicate or generative order have been explained by a Buddhist monk and scholar Hanh with a lot more clarity in capturing their subtleties. His explanation is:

> The British nuclear physicist David Bohm proposed the terms "explicate order" and "implicate order" to describe what Buddhist teachings call ordinary and ultimate reality. In the explicate order, everything exists outside of everything else. The elephant exists outside of the rose, the table exists outside of the forest, you exist outside of me, and so on. The explicate order is what we see when we don't look into things very deeply. But, as Bohm discovered, when we look more deeply into the nature of each so-called elementary particle, we see that one particle is made of all other particles. The notions we use in our daily life can no longer be applied in the domain of the infinitely small. In one particle, you can identify the existence of all other particles. Looking deeply into the nature of a particle reveals to us the implicate order, where everything is inside of everything else. – Hanh 2008: 82

However, Bohm's concept of implicate order has been compared with the Sāṁkhya–Yoga philosophy. This is stated in the following quotation:

> A Bohmian deterministic interpretation which argues for a non-local implicate order that is determinative of the manifest explicate order. Clearly, Sāṁkhya–Yoga is most compatible with a Bohmian interpretation that would argue for an all-pervasive (non-local) physicalist (*mūla-prakṛti*) or *citta* that is an unmanifest (*avyakta*) yet determinative implicate order that is constantly supporting or generating the explicate order or in other words the "manifest" (*vyakta*) world of ordinary awareness.
>
> – Larson 2003: 186

In the context of awareness, the contribution of the Sāṁkhya–Yoga philosophy is something unique. In that, the following observation is the most important:

> In addition to the physicalist intentionalities of awareness (*citta*) which are at the base of both the implicate and explicate orders of the physical world, there is a non-intentional pure contentless consciousness (*Puruṣa*) that provides the warrant not only for quantum observership but for communal communication and the system of life itself. It is essential witness (*sākṣī*) whose simple all-pervasive presence allows everything to be, and like the hologram it is present in its entirety in every self-awareness (hence *Puruṣa bahutva*). – Ibid.: 187

Consciousness and Implicate Order

We have dealt above mainly the material process in terms of the implicate order. "But the consciousness happens to be much more of the implicate order than that of matter" (Bohm and Peat 1987: 185). It may be stated that the consciousness has been captured by Bohm through the thought process, which is definitely in the implicate order.

> The very word implicate, meaning enfolded, suggests that one thought enfolds another and that a train of thought is actually a process of enfoldment of a succession of implications. – Ibid.

However, consciousness is organized through a generative order, which is more or less similar to the totality of the generative and implicate order that organizes matter (Bohm and Peat 1987: 186).

In order to know that how consciousness and matter are related, there are two possibilities:

i. to regard them as two generative and implicate orders, like separate but parallel streams that interrelate in some way (ibid.), and
ii. to treat them only as one order, whose ground includes the holomovement and may go beyond (ibid.).

Consciousness and Matter

There are two opposite views regarding consciousness:

i. held by many neuroscientists that "consciousness is an epiphenomenon of the brain"; and
ii. the opposite view is that "consciousness is a pure disembodied spirit in some kind of interaction with matter" (ibid.: 210).

However, Bohm has evolved an alternative view, which is stated below:

> Based on the notion that reality is inexhaustible and whatever we say a thing is, it is something more and also something different. Hence, for example, if we say that consciousness is a material process, this may well be fairly accurate up to a point. But it is also more. Its ground is the infinite depths of the implicate and generative orders, going from the relatively manifest on to ever greater subtlety.
> – Ibid.: 210

Now let us see how consciousness and matter are interconnected in the quantum field theory of physics.

Interconnection between Consciousness and Matter

It has been shown earlier that existence of an electron particle as well as electron wave is complementary in the quantum field theory of physics. This paves the way for an essential link between consciousness and the primary field. It may be noted that

> the fundamental realities of the primary field and consciousness are inseparable aspects of the same underlying process.
>
> – Bhaumik 2005: 176

It has been observed:

> David Bohm has named this underlying process the *implicate order*. Basil Hiley suggests: "Mind and matter are but different projections from this deeper implicate order, where such a division does not exist." He also emphasizes that "the implicate order is not some woolly metaphysical construction, it is a precise description of the underlying process," which is supported by credible mathematical analysis. – Ibid.

However, it has been further explained:

> In pre-space, the potentialities of consciousness and the primary field are united through mutual participation on a universal scale. Put another way, the essence of the implicate order is the one *source* that enfolds both the primary field (the common source of at least everything physical) and consciousness. Based on this thesis, it would be logical to infer that *the one source of the world's great spiritual traditions is grounded in the scientific reality*. – Ibid.: 117

The net energy of the universe happens to be zero. Therefore, the universe must have also started from the value of zero. In this context, it has been observed:

> The late visionary physicist David Bohm did not stop at zero. He conceived of something transcending zero and named it the implicate order which consists of the concurrent existence of all potentialities in the multidimensional pre-space. ... He suggests that material reality and consciousness are projections from this implicate order. – Ibid.: 196-97

Bohm has also evolved the concept of "holomovement" with a view to capture dynamic phenomenon of which all forms of the material universe flow.

> The aim of his approach is to study the order enfolded in this

> holomovement not by dealing with the structure of objects, but rather with the structure of movement, thus taking into account both the unity and the dynamic nature of the universe. According to Bohm, space and time emerge as forms flowing out of the holomovement: they too are infolded in its order.
>
> – Capra 1989: 353

That apart, the other fact is that

> the universal inter-connectedness of things and events, however, seems to be a fundamental feature of the atomic reality which does not depend on a particular interpretation of the mathematical theory. – Ibid.: 149

This is explained by David Bohm as follows:

> One is led to a new notion of unbroken wholeness which denies the celestial idea of analysability of the world into separately and independently existing parts. ... We have reversed the usual classical notion that the independent elementary parts of the world are the fundamental reality, and that the various systems are merely particular contingent forms and arrangements of these parts. Rather, we say that inseparable quantum interconnectedness of the whole universe is the fundamental reality and that relatively independently behaving parts are merely particular and contingent forms within the whole.
>
> – Ibid.: 149-50

Observer in Quantum Physics

It is stated:

> Quantum physics does not recognize an objective world independent of the subject who observes. The observer in the act of observation influences the thing observed and substantially alters it. We cannot observe anything in Nature without influencing and altering it. – Panda 2008: 96

In quantum physics, the observer in a real sense, the part of the experiment. However, "the Copenhagen interpretation puts much emphasis on the consciousness of the observer" (Panda 2008: 97). In this context, it is pointed out that "Einstein was a better critic of the Copenhagen interpretation of Niels Bohr" (ibid.: 97-98).

Einstein did not accept the notion of quantum theory. He assumed:

> The physical world exists independently of the human observer. Heisenberg criticized this notion of Einstein and called it "dogmatic" or "metaphysical" realism. He said: Quantum theory does not allow a completely objective description of Nature.
>
> – Ibid.: 98

The Copenhagen interpretation of quantum mechanics has accepted the physical world as an idea of the observer, but it does not consider the physical world as non-material. The physical world is perceived: "But we cannot be sure that our description conforms to the suchness of the world" (ibid.: 99).

It may, however, be reassuringly to be told:

> In atomic physics, the scientist cannot play the role of a detached objective observer, but becomes involved in the world he observes to the extent that he influences the properties of the observed objects. John Wheeler sees this involvement of the observer as the most important feature of quantum theory and he has, therefore, suggested replacing the word "observer" by the word "participator".
>
> – Capra 1989: 153

This has been explained by Wheeler himself:

> Nothing is more important about the quantum principle than this, that it destroys the concept of the world as "sitting out there"; with the observer safely separated from it by a 20 cm slab of plate glass. Even to observe so miniscule an object as an electron, he must shatter the glass. He must reach in. He must install his chosen measuring equipment. It is up to him to decide whether he shall measure position or momentum. To install the equipment to measure the one prevents and excludes his installing the equipment to measure the other. Moreover, the

> measurement changes the state of the electron. The universe will never afterwards be the same. To describe what has happened, one has to cross out that old word "observer" and put in its place the new word "participator". In some strange sense the universe is a participator's universe. – Capra 1989: 153

Emerging Implications

The main highlights emerging from the above observations of the quantum theory of physics are stated below:

i. The concept of causality does not seem to be undermined in the quantum physics. It is rather explained in different ways.
ii. Consciousness is treated as an essential feature of the holomovement in the quantum theory. This has become the important force as compared to the implicate order emerging from the matter. It may, however, be stated that Einstein by bringing the observer in the General Theory of Relativity has revolutionized the concept of space and time and put an end to the idea of absolute time which is advocated by Aristotle and Newton. Time and space have become relative concepts. This is mainly because of the observer, which happens to be a self-conscious human being.
iii. Self-consciousness of human being has become the source of nature in the sense that the physical world is known by self-consciousness. This may be supported by the following observation based on the Indian philosophy of Vedic Vision of Consciousness and reality.
iv. All these transmutations that matter has undergone during the last one to two centuries are obviously a work of human consciousness. It is consciousness which broke the tangible chunk of matter into ordinarily invisible atoms, and the latter into absolutely invisible particles. Again, it is consciousness which saw particles as sheer quanta of energy constantly in a state of flux and unpredictable in regard to its position and

> velocity. Had the scientists' consciousness not been involved in this act of transformation, matter must still have remained only in chunks, both big and small. – Singh 2004: 2

David Bohm's Views on Consciousness and Matter

According to Bohm,

> matter and consciousness are manifestations of implicate order, which enfolds all that which is. We may remark that this is strikingly similar to the Vedāntic notion, in light of which contradiction between mind and body is resolved. – Joshi 2006: 26

In casual interpretation of the field theory, there are two implicate orders: the first implicate order is the field itself and the second implicate order is obtained by the super-quantum wave function (Bohm and Peat 1987: 182). However, in an order of unfoldment, it is mentioned:

> If there are higher implicate orders, then a similar generative order will prevail throughout all the levels. Ultimately, it is, of course, the holomovement, and what may lie beyond, from which all is generated. – Ibid.: 184

The concept of implicate order has, however, been compared with Sāṁkhya–Yoga's concept of *mūla-prakṛti* or *citta* that is an unmanifest (*avyakta*), yet determinative implicate order which is constantly generating the explicate order or in other words the manifest (*vyakta*) world of ordinary awareness (Larson 2003: 186). Against this manifestation there is pure contentless consciousness (*Puruṣa*), being the essential witness (*sākṣī*) whose simple presence "allows everything to be, and like the hologram it is present in its entirety in every self-awareness (hence *Puruṣa bahutva*)" (ibid.: 187).

According to Bohm and Peat, consciousness happens to partake much more of the implicate order than that of matter (1987: 185). Consciousness is captured by the thought process which is definitely the implicate order. The word implicate means enfolded. It suggests that one thought enfolds another (ibid.). However, the main approach adopted by Bohm and Peat (1987: 211-12) regarding consciousness is given below:

i. Consciousness has two aspects: (a) material, and (b) mental. The material aspect can be studied scientifically. But the mental aspect would be rather difficult to capture by scientific studies. Therefore, one has to go beyond the usual approaches in which the mind and the matter are two separate but interacting streams.

ii. The root of the manifestation lies in the ultimate depths of the implicate and generative orders of the totality of matter, life and mind. In this context, it has been observed that "*even inanimate matter must have some kind of mental aspect*" (emphasis added by italics).

iii. There is no absolutely sharp "cut" or break between consciousness, life and matter whether animate or inanimate. Therefore, it has been concluded that as the consciousness approached to its origin of generative order, the mental aspect becomes more important, "while in the journey of 'downstream', the manifest physical side becomes more evident".

Now the question arises of how the mental side of consciousness is related to the material side of consciousness. The relationship between both aspects is tried to be established through awareness and attention.

Awareness and Attention

Consciousness has been treated as the total state of "knowingness" of the individual. Therefore, the term "conscious awareness" is taken to mean a consciousness (i.e. a knowingness). It is also stated that consciousness is only a small part of the total field of consciousness or knowingness (ibid.: 214). Whereas,

> the word attention means literally stretching the mind toward something. This implies an inner activity that is needed to

> grasp the object of interest mentally. Even physically it has been demonstrated that a kind of attention must operate, as for example, in the eye's scanning pattern, which varies according to each person's concept of the object that is being looked at.
>
> – Bohm and Peat 1987: 214-15

In this context, it has been stated that the movement of attention along with the sensitivity of awareness is constantly bringing the content of physical side to the "mental" side. In this way, a relationship between the physical side and the mental side has been established in consciousness. However, in the context of an interconnection between consciousness and matter, Bohm has stated that like mind and matter, both are interdependent and correlated to each other, but not causally connected (Capra 1989: 353).

4

Substantiality and Causality

Introduction

It is rather a well-known fact that substance and its cause have always been recognized in metaphysics and ontology of both the Eastern and Western philosophy. Yet, the concept of causality is the most puzzling aspect of philosophy mainly because of very divergent views among different schools of philosophy. Therefore, before presenting the concept of causality followed in different philosophies, an attempt is made below to provide a brief overview of causality.

Causality: An Overview

Causation has been recognized as a metaphysical entity by Aristotle: for, he is in search of the first and final cause of the universe. In this context, it is stated:

> Human and cosmic production is of the same nature, and, human causation at work is an exemplar of cosmic becoming. Aristotle finds that in human production, e.g. of a chair there are four kinds of causes at work simultaneously, namely *material*, *efficient*, *formal* and *final* causes. For example, in making a chair there is the wood which may be called the *material* cause. Again, there is the skill and instruments through which a carpenter builds a chair. This may be called the *efficient* cause. Here energy, skill, instrument and the power are included. Then comes the *formal* cause which means the shape, the design and the kind of chair which has to be made. Lastly there is *final* purpose for which chair has to be made. – Masih 2002: 93

The above four kinds of cause have been combined into a consistent form of philosophical explanation of the world. Further, these four kinds of cause are reduced by Aristotle to *form* and *matter* for explaining the world. Both are inseparable.

It may be noted that the terms "form" and "matter" are quite fluid. For example,

> wood is matter in relation to the chair, which is its form. But "wood" is again form in relation to a growing tree. From another stand, one can say that matter is bare possibility of becoming its "various form". For example "wood" is the possibility which can be actualized into chair, table, doors or windows. – Masih 2002: 95

This shows that "form" and "matter" are fluid and relative. However, form and matter are inseparable, but they can be distinguished only in thought.

Schopenhauer has also treated the matter as causality. This is stated below:

> For matter is absolutely nothing but causality. ... Its being is its acting: it is not possible to conceive for it any other being. Only as something acting does it fill space and time; its action on the immediate object (which is itself matter) conditions the perception in which alone it exists. The consequence of the action of every material object on another is known only insofar as the latter now acts on the immediate object in a way different from that in which it acted previously; it consists in this alone. Thus cause and effect are the whole essence and nature of matter. ... Its whole being and essence consist only in the orderly and regular change produced by one part of it in another; consequently, its being and essence are entirely relative. – Cross 2014: 63

Similar is the case with Indian philosophy, under which the different notions are treated as substance, which is related to cause. For instance, the Vaiśeṣika philosophy, *samavāya* (inherence) is the sixth category of *padārtha* (substance). It is treated as the relation between cause and effect. This has been defined by Praśastapāda as,

> The relationship subsisting among things that are inseparable, standing to one another in the relation of the container and the contained, and being the basis of the idea, this is in that.
>
> – Radhakrishnan 2002: 216

It may be further stated:

> The relation which binds a substance and its qualities, a whole and its parts, motion and the object in motion, the individual and universe, cause and effect, is that of *samavāya* (inherence).
>
> – Ibid.: 217

In the Sāṁkhya philosophy also, *Prakṛti* happens to be the causal background of all objective world. *Prakṛti* alone is the substantive cause.

The concept of causality in different philosophies is briefly stated below:

i. The cause–effect relationship in the West is the effect–cause relationship in India. The difference may be due to the customary chronological orientation in the West and the ontological orientation in India. Causality or causation is effectuality or resultness in India (Organ 1988: 72).

   In the Indian context, the internal conviction about the truth of the principle of causality is that there is no phenomenon without its cause. This is mainly because it is derived from "one of the innate tendencies or *saṁskāra* inherent in mind is generated by its past experiences" (Woodroffe 2001: 253-54). Whereas, according to Kant, it is the persistent reality of the causal order, which is a necessary assumption for our knowledge of the external world as time and space (ibid.: 254). These observations show that in Indian context, causality is based upon the more fundamental notion of continuity (ibid.: 273). Whereas, in Kant's philosophy, it is a necessary assumption.

ii. The causality in Indian philosophy has relationship with both real and unreal. It is mainly due to the fact that the question has been asked about the causality, whether it is real (*sat*) or non-real (*asat*). As a result, the causality has been interpreted in two ways: (a) Asatkāraṇavāda, the unreal cause theory; and (b) Satkāryavāda, the real effect theory.

The Sāṁkhya theory of causation is known as Satkāryavāda. The view of causality of Advaita Vedānta also happens to be Satkāryavāda, although at some places it has been mentioned as Satkāraṇavāda. However, the Vaiśeṣika theory of causality is known as Asatkāryavāda; i.e. the unreal effect theory. It may be noted that all these theories will be discussed in this chapter.

iii. An extreme view about causality is that

> an object cannot exist, unless it is thought of ... and two thoughts cannot occur simultaneously. If, however, we grant for argument's sake that objects could exist independently of their being cognized, we should still be unable to allow the relation of cause and effect. Strictly speaking, it is only after the occurrence that we can take it to be the effect of a cause, by which time the ostensible cause must be presumed to have passed over entirely into effect, the two never having been observed in concert. *Causality is, therefore, a meaningless concept* (emphasis added by italics).
> – Levy 2004: 55-56

This observation does not seem to be correct for the obvious reason that Śaṅkara (founder of Advaita Vedānta) has clearly stated that "(cause and effect are non-different) since the effect is perceived when the cause is there" (Swami Gambhirananda 2000: 335, v. II.1.15). But it is not otherwise. In such a situation, where is the question of two thoughts, the basis of which the causality has been treated as a meaningless concept.

Since the Vedāntic theory of causation is originally traced to Sāṁkhya system (Rangaswami 2012: 241), an attempt has been made below to clarify certain issues raised above on the basis of Sāṁkhya's concept of causal series. In this context, the following observation deserves attention:

> A moment cannot be thought of as containing any parts standing in the relation of antecedence and sequence. "If change is represented by Time-series, a moment as the unit of time may be supposed to represent the unit of change. Now all physical change may be reduced to the motion of atoms in space, and we may therefore define the moment as representing the ultimate unit of such change – viz. the (instantaneous) transit of an atom (or rather a *tanmātra*) from one point in space to the next succeeding point. Even an atom has constituent parts (the *tanmātras*), and hence an atom must take more than one moment to change its position. The motion of that which is absolutely simple and without parts from one point in space to the next must be instantaneous, and conceived as absolute unit of change (and therefore of time, *kṣaṇa*). .... Order in Time is nothing but the relation of antecedence and sequence between the moment that is and that went just before. – Seal 1985: 19-20

This shows that the theory of causation is not a meaningless concept as mentioned above.

However,

> causation, which involves duality (the creator and the created) does not hold water in the light of Advaita ultimately, but as in the case of his other philosophical concepts, causation has to be logically explained at the empirical level. – Rangaswami 2012: 241

iv. It may be noted that in the Absolute Reality the causality did not exist at all, but in the empirical world it has an important role to play. This is evident from the following observation:

> The empirical world gradually comes into being for the infant, beginning with its mother and immediate surroundings. By conceiving every change of sensations as

> an effect and referring this to a cause, the understanding brings about the cerebral phenomenon of the objective world, and so it is only when understanding begins to act ... only when the understanding applies its sole form, the law of causality, that a powerful transformation takes place whereby subjective sensation becomes objective intuitive perception. – Cross 2014: 61

However, it is quite important to state that even, "matter is only the objective correlative of the understanding; it is causality itself objectively conceived" (ibid.: 63).

This view is in conformity with the Sāṁkhya in which *prakr̥ti* is treated as causal background of all objective world. How the concept of causality is treated in the philosophies of Hume and Kant will also be examined in this chapter; so that one may get a better perspective about causality.

Vaiśeṣika Theory of Causation

The most important aspects of Vaiśeṣika philosophy are:

i. the concept *adr̥ṣṭa* (unseen) happens to be the universal force responsible for the first motion in the primordial atoms at the beginning of creation;
ii. the world as an effect produced by the aggregation of the cause – the ultimate atom; and
iii. *saṁskāra* (impression) generates a series of motion.

However, the theory of causation of Vaiśeṣika philosophy is known as Asatkāryavāda (the unreal effect theory). This is evident from the following observation:

> It claims that non-existence of effect follows from non-existence of cause, but non-existence of cause does not follow from the non-existence of the effect. An effect has only a temporary existence. Before its production, and after its destruction it is non-existent. Hence the world, which is an effect, is not an appearance (*vivarta*)

> of the cause, nor an evolution (*pariṇāma*), but is produced by the aggregation of the cause – the ultimate atom. – Safaya 1976: 164

MOTION

According to the commentary on Vaiśeṣika aphorisms, motion (*karma*) is defined as the unconditional cause of change in a particle. In simplest form it is instantaneous and distinguished from *vega* (impressioned motion-momentum), which has persistent tendency, *saṁskāra*, implying thereby a series of motions. In this context it is stated:

> In one and the same particle there can be only one motion, (*karma*) at any given moment, since its change of place at that moment is one and definite. ... The supposition of two (instantaneous) motions in the same particle is superfluous. They may be so opposed as to neutralize each other in which case the particle would be at rest. – Seal 1985: 129

However, motion is always marked by certain direction. The successive motions of a particle may be in the same direction or upward and downward, or other forms of rectilinear motion, contraction, dilation. "The direction of the successive motions may be different, as in curvilinear motion" (ibid.: 130).

MOTION IN RELATION TO ITS CAUSES

Movements which are not caused by contact with matter are given below:

1. Movements caused by volition, e.g. the movement of hand.
2. Movement of a falling body is caused by gravity. This happens to the attraction (pulling force) exercised by the earth on a material body (ibid.: 131-32).
3. Motion of fluids as the downward flow in a stream. This is due fluidity, which is a characteristic property of certain kinds of atoms, in some cases original, in others produced by the contact of these atoms with the atomic particles of heat (ibid.: 132).

4. Certain motions are not due to material contact, but their mechanical causes are unknown. This may be ascribed to *adṛṣṭa* (Seal 1985: 132).

ADṚṢṬA

It is observed:

> Final causality or motion is attributed by the First Standard to *adṛṣṭa* (unseen) which is resorted to in explanation of observed phenomena only when these cannot be derived in any way from the operation of known causes. – Woodroffe 2001: 257

Several classes of cases fall under *adṛṣṭa* are given below (Seal 1985: 133):

i. The operation of merit and demerit, a transcendental cause, which has to be posited in explaining the conjunctions and disconjunctions of souls within their organic vehicles.
ii. Various kinds of motions in the different classes of elements, e.g. their natural modes of operation, such as the dispersion of *vāyu* (air, gas), the upward motion of fire, the attraction of the needle by the magnet, etc. motion which serve the ends of creation and created beings.

However, there are certain motions, which are produced by contact. Such motions are stated below (ibid.: 134-36):

1. Motion due to direct contact with a body exercising continued pressure, e.g. the motion of an object pushed or pulled by hand, the motion of the mud under having stones, the motion of the arrow due to the pressure exercised by the bow string.
2. Motion due to direct contact for an instant with a body that strikes and produces an impact, e.g. in the case of a stone falling against a hard object.
3. Motion due to direct contact with an elastic body which exercises a moving force by means of its elasticity in the act of restitution of the original form, e.g. the motion of low-string due to the force exercised by the piece of bamboo.

4. Motion due to contact with a body which is itself in contact with another possesses *vega* (impressed motion or momentum).

Persistent tendency is of two kinds:

a. persistent tendency to motion in a moving body, and
b. the tendency to restitution of shape in an elastic body.

CONCEPT OF VEGA

A motion (*karma*) is conceived as change of place in particle, which is incapable of producing another motion,

> but the pressure, impact or other force which produces the first motion produces through that motion a *saṁskāra* or persistent tendency to motion (*vega*) which is the cause of continued motion in a straight line, i.e. in the direction of the first motion.
>
> – Seal 1985: 137

It may be further noted:

> *Vega*, it will be seen, corresponds to inertia in some respects, and to momentum (impressed motion) in others. This is the nearest approach to Newton's First Law of Motion in the Vaiśeṣika theory of motion.
>
> – Ibid.

Impressed notion (*vega*) has tendency to move on in a straight line. It is counteracted by contact with tangible objects. However, *vega* (momentum) also "produces work in opposition to the resisting force, and thereby becomes weaker and weaker until it comes to an end" (ibid.: 138).

CAUSES OF PRESSURE AND OF IMPACT

It is observed that pressure is produced by impressed *vega*, elasticity, gravity, fluidity or volition, i.e. "the *vega* of the wind produces pressure on grass, that of a current water" (ibid.). Whereas, gravity with contact produces pressure on earth.

Impact is produced by contact with a body possessing *vega*

> (impressed motion), where the contact is instantly followed by disjunction (or rebounding). If the contact continues, the result is pressure.
> – Seal 1985: 138

The most important aspect of Vaiśeṣika theory of causation is that the non-existence of effect prior to its origination. The non-existence has been accepted as category. This has been objected by the Sāṁkhya system, in which it is categorically stated that the effect does exist in the cause. The Sāṁkhya theory of causation is discussed below.

Sāṁkhya Theory of Causation

There are two ultimate principles *Puruṣa* and *Prakṛti* as derived by the transcendental analysis of the structure of experience. *Puruṣa* is pure consciousness. *Prakṛti* is the causal background of all objective world. Its existence is through the application of the principal causality.

> The theory that the effect really exists before hand in its cause is one of the central features of the Sāṁkhya system. The Sāṁkhya defines cause as the entity in which the effect subsists in a latent form.
> – Radhakrishnan 2002: 256

This is known as Satkāryavāda (the real effect theory). It "is contrary to Ārambhavāda held by those who accept non-existence as separate category" (Ram 1995: 86). However, the Sāṁkhya theory of Satkāryavāda is justified on the following grounds:

i. Non-existence cannot be brought into existence by anybody, "for, not even thousands of artists can ever change blue (colour) to yellow" (Swami Virupakshananda 2003: 31, *kā* 56). An effect can only be produced by material cause.
ii. All effects are not producible from all causes (ibid.: 30).
iii. The efficient cause can produce only that for which it is efficient (ibid.: 33).
iv. Effect is of the same essence as the cause. "The cloth is not different from the yarns" (ibid.).

OBJECTION

The Naiyāyikas have raised an objection against the above theory of causation by stating that, "it suffers from the absurdity of establishing what is already established" (Swami Virupakshananda 2003: 30). This is known as *siddha sādhana doṣa*, meaning thereby that the effect is already existent.

ANSWER

> The causal efficacy belongs to destruction (*pradhvaṁsa* as it is pure negation); causal efficacy belongs only to positive entities consisting of component particles of the seed (and lump of clay). If it were possible that a positive entity is produced from mere negation, then, such negation being easily available everywhere, the absurd possibility that all things could be produced at all places would arise.
> – Ibid.: 30-31

It may, however, be noted that several objections have been raised against the Sāṁkhya theory of causation (Satkāryavāda). More or less similar types of arguments have been given against various objections. These objections and answers are stated in quite details in the *Sāṁkhya-Kārikā* of Īśvarakr̥ṣṇa with the *Tattvakaumudī* of Vācaspati Miśra and the *Yuktidīpikā* as mentioned in *Encyclopedia of Indian Philosophies* vol. IV by Larson and Bhattacharya (1987). These books may be consulted for details about objections and answers regarding Satkāryavāda of the Sāṁkhya system. However, the most arguments in justifying Satkāryavāda are stated below:

i. (1) Some say (Buddhist assent) the existent (*effect*) emanates from the non-existent (cause). (2) Others (Advaitins) affirm that all effects are merely illusory appearances of One Reality and are not real entities by themselves. (3) Others (like Kaṇāda and Gautama) hold that the (previously) *non-existent effect* (arises) from the *existent cause*. Lastly, (4) the ancients (like Kapila) declare that *existent* (effect) emanates from the *existent* (cause) (Swami Virupakshananda 2003: 29, *kā* 56).

ii. In reality, there can be no production for what is non-existent and no destruction for what is existent. This has been declared to be so by Bhagavān Kṛṣṇa Dvaipāyana (in *Bhagavadgītā* II.16); there is no being for the non-existent nor non-being for the existent (Swami Virupakshananda 2003: 35).

According to Sāṁkhya theory, the effect is originally existent in material cause prior to its manifestation (Catalina 1968: 25). This is further explained below:

> The cause evolves into the effect and yet as cause, remains what it is. As effect it is modified that is the effect is the cause modified. All which exists is a transformation of one substance, their cause. Causation is transformation: cause and effect being different positions of the same thing in the time sequence, the antecedent position being the cause and the consequent position the effect.
>
> – Woodroffe 2001: 208

The Sāṁkhya theory of causation has been summed up very well in a statement that "the effect and the cause are explicit and implicit states of the same substance".[1] This may be explained by the example of cloth which is not actually different from the thread from which it is made. It is, thus, evident that the effect exists in the material cause prior to its production as mentioned above.

However, it is observed:

> If all effects are latent in their cause, and if infinite regress is to be avoided, there must be an uncaused cause. From the principle of causality it is deduced that the ultimate basis of empirical universe is the unmanifested (*avyaktam*) *prakṛti*.
>
> – Radhakrishnan 2002: 259

PRAKṚTI

The unmanifested *prakṛti* has been justified on the basis of *Sāṁkhya-Kārikā* 15 and 16. This is based on the following grounds:

---

1 This is quoted by Catalina 1968: 26. It is based on Chatterjee and Dutta 1950: 260.

i. The finite nature of objects is limited and dependent on something which is more enduring and pervasive. "The finite as finite, therefore, cannot be the source of the universe".

ii. All individual things possess certain pervasive characteristics, which are common source to all.

iii. Evolution takes place due to the efficiency of the cause. "There is an active principle manifesting itself in the development of things".

iv. There is differentiation between the cause and the effect. Therefore, we cannot say that the finite and conditioned world has its own cause.

v. There is the obvious unity of the universe, suggesting a single cause. The Sāṁkhya assumes the continuity of the world from the lowest to the highest. The products evolve and dissolve in a definite order. The world is said to be the *pariṇāma* (transformation), of *prakṛti,* which is its cause" (Radhakrishnan 2002: 259).

It may, however, be stated that *prakṛti* has been treated as *dharmī* in *Yogasūtra* III.14 of Patañjali. This *sūtra* is translated into English as:

> The substratum is that in which the properties – latent, active or unmanifest – inhere. – Taimni 1999: 304

The commentary on this *sūtra* is stated below:

> All properties of different elements, whether manifest or unmanifest, are considered to inhere in and to be derived from one substratum which is called *dharmī.* This substratum which is the root of all properties is none other than *prakṛti.* When a particular property disappears we may say that it has become latent in *prakṛti.* When it becomes manifest we may say that it has taken an active form in *prakṛti.* – Ibid.

It, thus, emerges that there are two ways to understand *prakṛti* the unmanifest and the manifest forms. The former is reverse of the latter. The unmanifest *prakṛti* is without cause, eternal, pervasive and inactive.

> Even though the unmanifest possesses the activity of evolution, yet there is no mobility in it. The unmanifest is, therefore, one, not a component, non-mergent, unconjunct and independent.
> – Swami Virupakshananda 2003: 39-40

Whereas, the manifest *prakṛti* is

> producible, non-eternal, non-pervasive, active, multiform, dependent serving as a mark (of inference), aggregate of parts and subordinate. – Ibid.: 38

Advaita Vedānta

The causality has been denied by Vedānta from the ontological standpoint, but its existence is accepted at empirical level. Śaṅkara has stated that the effect is non-different from the cause because it is perceived when the cause is there, but not otherwise (Swami Gambhirananda 2000: 335, v. II.1.15). In other words, the effect must pre-exist in its cause, and if it does not pre-exist in cause, it can never arise from it. In this context, it may be stated that oil can be pressed out of oil seeds only: for, it pre-exists in them. So the effect pre-exists in its cause as not different before its own origin. This fact should be understood that "the effect must be non-different from the cause even after its birth" (ibid.: 337, v. II.1.16).

The above arguments resemble the theory of Satkāryavāda of the Sāṁkhya philosophy as discussed earlier. However,

> the Advaitins support Satkāryavāda according to which the material cause and the effect are not two different things but something in two different states – the potential and the actual. For example, the clay is the potential state of the pot and the pot is the actual state of the clay. The potential state or the subtle state is the causal state of the thing and the actual or the gross state is its effect state. – Bhattacharyya 1992: 120

This theory of Satkāryavāda has been interpreted in another way.

It is observed that "Śaṅkara advocates Satkāryavāda in the form of Vivartavāda. The effect is the appearance (*vivarta*) of the cause. The cause is real; the effect is unreal" (Sinha 2006: 544).

In view of the above facts, some Advaita scholars have interpreted it in different ways. This is evident from the following observations:

> Advaita Vedānta considers the causal substance alone as real and the apparent forms as mere illusory appearances, not having any existence of their own. This perspective is known as Satkāraṇavāda, the theory that cause is the reality, which was preferred by Śaṅkara. Rāmānuja, the proponent of the Viśiṣṭādvaita school of Vedānta, on the other hand, considered both the substance and the apparent forms as eal. His stand is known as Satkāryavāda, the theory that the effect is also real.
>
> – Prasad 1999: 141

However, another argument is that the every causal process must have an agent. This has been referred to as both complex and difficult for a Western scientific mind to sympathize with such argument (Potter 1998: 65). In this context, it is stated:

> Creation is an act, which like motion, etc. must have an agent. It is a contradiction in terms that there can be an act but not an agent. – Swami Gambhirananda 2000: 342, v. II.1.18

The activity of the causal agent transforms the cause into the shape of the effect.

> An unrolled cloth pre-exists in a rolled cloth. An agent's activity merely unfolds the rolled cloth and spreads it out.[2]

It emerges that it is the agent who is responsible for the nature of effect. But "if the effect does not exist before origination, the creative action will be without any agent and without any reality" (Swami Gambhirananda 2000: 341-42, v. II.1.18). It means that

---

2 Sinha 2006: 543-44. This observation is based on Swami Gambhirananda 2000: 345-46, v. II.1.19.

> without an agent, an effect will be without a nature. But furthermore, Śaṅkara argues the only thing that can properly function as agent is the effect itself. It must, therefore, pre-exist its own manifestation, for nothing else can serve as agent.
>
> – Potter 1998: 66

The theory of the pre-existence of the effect in the cause may be explained on the basis of *Chāndogya Upaniṣad* VI.2.1. The question was about one substratum underlying everything in all the worlds. That substance in this stanza happens to be *sat* meaning thereby "the Real", "the Being", "the Existence". The *sat* is conceived as causal to everything. This is evident from the following observation:

> This *sat* never exists as pure *sat* with no assumed, apparent, transient form of the world, even as the existence of gold always is in the form of some transitory form of ornaments, coins and the like. Likewise, no transitory apparent form can exist in the absence of the underlying eternal substance either. This inseparable oneness of cause and effect, of the eternal and the transient, of *Brahman* and the world, is what the original words *ekam eva advitīyam* (the one without a second alone) signify.
>
> – Prasad 2006a: 405

It may be stated that the Vedāntic theory of causation implies six requisites according to Sureśvara. These requisites are given below (Grimes 1992: 13-14):

i. The cause and effect relationship is in terms of succession; the cause is always earlier and the effect is always later.
ii. The cause always precedes the effect and never vice versa.
iii. The relationship between the cause and the effect is a necessary relationship and not a contingent one.
iv. The cause and the effect are not completely identical nor are they totally different.
v. The relationship between the cause and the effect is a one-sided relationship. The effect is always dependent upon the cause and never vice versa.

vi. Between the cause and the effect, the cause alone is real.

In view of the above requisites, it is stated:

> Any theory of causation is impossible. From the seeming reality of a causal relationship at an empirical level, one is led to the discovery that, philosophically speaking, there cannot be a logical causal relationship. – Grimes 1992: 14

Therefore, Vivartavāda seems to be the central teaching of Advaita Vedānta. This has been referred to earlier. Yet, it may be reassuring to be told that

> the Absolute is real; the world is non-real; the individual and the Absolute are not different. Or again, the central teaching of Advaita is conveyed in the verse. The Individual and the Absolute are one. – Ibid.: 14-15

Philosophy of Bauddha Dharma

THE CAUSAL THEORY OF CO-PRODUCTION

The theory of dependent origination (*pratītya-samutpāda*) is interpreted as the causal theory of co-production, indicating thereby that the entities arise due to mutual dependence and all phenomena are conditioned, viz. interdependent. In this context, the following observation is important:

> This formulation of causality in terms of interdependence allows the Buddha to restrict its field of operation to the phenomenal realm. It satisfactorily explains the content of temporal relations. The relations, which occur in a sequential order, are not inferred rationally, but are seen as having their source in how the temporal becoming is experienced. The "this" denotes the cause, whereas "that" is the effect of the cause. Prior to the emergence of the effect, it is the cause that is experienced by each one of us. If the cause is absent, then there would be no effect, which would denote the cessation of becoming. Thus the positive and negative aspects of the causal formula (when this, then that; when not this, then not that) are meant to strengthen the argument

> concerning the relational nature of cause and effect. Also the intention of the formula in general is to explain the relativity as well as the genetic character of causality. The statement "when this is, that comes to be" expresses relative or dependent nature of cause and effect, which means in the absence of cause no effect is eventuated. Likewise no possibility exists for the existence of cause in the absence of effect. – Pandit 2008: 108

The theory of dependent origination (*pratītya-samutpāda*) of Buddhism is shown in Table 4.1:

Table 4.1: The Theory of Dependent Origination in Buddhism

	Dependent Origination	*Life*	*Process of Existence*
1.	Dependent on ignorance arises kammic formations	Past	*Karma*
2.	Dependent on kammic formations arises consciousness		
3.	Dependent on consciousness arises mind and matter	Present	Rebirth
4.	Dependent on mind and matter arises the six sense bases		
5.	Dependent on six sense bases arises contact		
6.	Dependent on contact arises feeling		
7.	Dependent on feeling arises craving		
8.	Dependent on craving arises clinging		*Karma*
9.	Dependent on clinging arises existence		
10.	Dependent on existence arises birth		
11.	Dependent on birth arises decay and old age	Future	Rebirth
12.	Dependent on decay and old age arises death		

Sources: Bhikkhu Bodhi 1999: 301; Collins 1982: 204

This dependent origination is explained further as follows:

> The relationship between ignorance and suffering is causal, viz. one factor leading to the arising of other factor in the chain of causation till the factor of suffering is given rise to. It is said that ignorance terminates in the arising of formations, and formations

> give rise to consciousness. Likewise from consciousness arise name-and-form, from name-and-form arise six senses, from six senses arises contact, from contact arises sensation, from sensation arises craving, from craving arises grasping, from grasping arises becoming, from becoming arises birth, from birth arises old age and death, from old age and death arise grief, lamentation, dejection and despair. In this manner is explained the entire process of arising. It is the cycle of arising of one factor from the other that visualizes the scheme of co-arising. Opposite to arising is cessation. Upon the cessation of ignorance the arising of formation ceases and this process continues till the cessation of last factor, which is the cessation of old age and death. Upon the cessation of old age and death comes to standstill the arising of suffering. And this point of cessation is reached the nirvāṇic cessation or extinction. – Pandit 2008: 112

NĀGĀRJUNA'S VIEW OF CAUSALITY

The dependent origination has been interpreted as emptiness (*śūnyatā*) (Garfield 1995: 69, *kārikā* XXIV.18). This has been explained in the following way:

> This revolutionary view of Nāgārjuna establishes the fact that not only the world, but even the so-called co-arising has only conventional value. They are not real on account of them being devoid of intrinsic being. As to why the world as phenomenal entity is devoid of intrinsic being is because it is not "produced through any intrinsic being", and that is what co-arising means. What we normally call an entity is simply nothing but a conventional way of designating things and beings. All designated things are destitute of reality, which is to say that they lack intrinsic being. The absence of intrinsic being is equated with "emptiness". – Pandit 2008: 119

However, according to Nāgārjuna (Stcherbatsky 2003: 19) there can be only four views about causality. They are:

i. the theory of self-becoming (*svata-utpattiḥ*);
ii. production from another (*parata-utpattiḥ*);

iii. production from both, i.e. from itself and from another (*dvābhyām-utpattiḥ*); and

iv. production without any cause, production by chance (*ahetuta-utpattiḥ*).

These views are elaborated below.

The Theory of Self-becoming

This seems to be referred to Satkāryavāda of Sāṁkhya, in which the cause and the effect are indentical. It is criticized by Nāgārjuna (Stcherbatsky 2003: 19) on the following grounds:

a. It is stated that if the effect is already existing in the cause, no purpose would be served by its re-production. In this context, the Sāṁkhya reply would be that the effect may be present in the cause, but in its manifestation, it is something new. This difference, however, according to Nāgārjuna, would be against the identity of the underlying substratum.

b. If the cause is partly actual and partly potential, it would amount to accepting opposed natures in one and the same thing. If the cause is wholly potential, it cannot by itself become actual without an extraneous aid. The oil cannot be got out of the seed, unless it is pressed by a crusher. If it has to depend on an external aid, then there is no *svata upattiḥ* (self-production). This amounts to giving up Satkāryavāda.

c. If the cause and the effect are identical, it would be impossible to distinguish one as the producer of the other. The identity of the cause and the effect is, therefore, self-contradiction.

Production from Another

It indicates that the cause is different from the effect. This view is referred to as Asatkāryavāda. Nāgārjuna has criticized this view also because it is a heterogeneous view of causality (Stcherbatsky 2003: 19). The criticisms are stated below (ibid.: 20):

a. If the cause is different from the effect, the relation between the two cannot be established. In that case anything can be produced from anything.

b. If the effect is produced by a combination of factors, it requires another factor to coordinate it. This would lead to a *regressus ad infinitum.*

Production from Both

In this case, the effect is both identical with and different from the cause. "This is a combination of both Satkāryavāda and Asatkāryavāda and so contains the inconsistencies of both" (Stcherbatsky 2003: 20).

Production Without Any Cause

In this case, things are produced without a cause, by chance. If no reason is assigned, it amounts to dogmatism (ibid.).

Having criticized all the above views, Nāgārjuna has concluded that causality is mere a creation of thought, which is superimposed upon the objects.

SAUTRĀNTIKA'S VIEW OF CAUSALITY IN PERCEPTION

The Sautrāntikas have taken into account four causal factors, which are necessary for perceptual process in cognizing the objects. The combination of all the four causes is essential in the production of the effect. This is referred to as the entire causal complex (*sāmagrī*) in the Buddhist philosophy (Mookerjee 1993: 316). These four causes are explained below:

1. *Ālambana pratyaya*: "The *ālambana* is the causal basis, that is, the object of a particular state of consciousness, which is regarded as an effect or event" (Matilal 1997: 285). This is also referred to the relation between the object and the subject of perception (Chaudhury 1983: 114).
2. *Samānāntara pratyaya*: In the stream of thought, every preceding moment of consciousness becomes the cause of the succeeding moment. This gives rise to a momentary

homogeneous series, representing thereby the life continuum. In this context, it is observed that "*samānāntara pratyaya* is now replaced by the relation of the store-consciousness (*ālaya*) to its modification (*pariṇāma*)" (Stcherbatsky 2003: 38).

Ālaya-vijñāna is here a storehouse where the kārmic seeds (*bījas*) in the form of impressions (*vāsanās*) are stored up. This is evident from the following extract:

> It belongs to the phenomenal part of existence because all the results (*vipāka*) of *karma* are there stored up. This store-consciousness in this system occupies a position analogous to the primitive matter (*pradhāna*) of the Sāṁkhya school. All individual objects and ideas are regarded as its modifications (*pariṇāma*) by the Sāṁkhya. The Yogācāras likewise regard all separate ideas as modifications of their store-consciousness. This represents a disguised return from the theory of a stream of thought to the doctrine of substantial soul.
>
> – Ibid.: 37-38

3. *Sahakārī pratyaya*: "The auxiliary causes are rather cooperative factors, all acting together towards a common effect" (Mookerjee 1993: 317). Further, it is stated that

   > light, attention, etc. are the cooperative causes of sense perception, as the light reveals the object in a clear perspective and attention makes the cognition possible.
   >
   > – Ibid.: 318

4. *Adhipati pratyaya*: It is the decisive, dominating, ruling or specific condition, the reason (*kāraṇa*) for the arising of something else, that which seems to "generate" it (*jāṅka*), as sight-organ and sight-object for sight-consciousness or visual sensation, the seed for the sprout, etc. (Chaudhury 1983: 114).

In the manifestation of any phenomenon, all the above causes are required. It is stated:

> The cause as condition (*hetu pratyaya*) is the seed from which

> things arise, but nothing can arise from this alone. There also has to be a development condition (*adhipati pratyaya*), an object condition (*ālambana pratyaya*) and the condition of immediate continuity (*samānāntara pratyaya*).
> – Hanh 2008: 102

CAUSAL ASPECT OF ĀLAYA-VIJÑĀNA OF YOGĀCĀRA VIJÑĀNAVĀDA BUDDHISM

All kārmic seeds are stored in *ālaya-vijñāna*. Further, all phenomena originate from pure and impure elements, i.e. seeds are causally combined in *ālaya-vijñāna*.

The *ālaya-vijñāna* being the stream of consciousness is continuously flowing, it is neither permanent nor impermanent.

> From beginningless time it is born and perishes from moment to moment in an ever-changing manner. As cause it perishes, so it is not permanent; as effect it is born, so it is not impermanent. Thus, this consciousness is in perpetual evolution like a torent.
> – Ganguly 1992: 26

In the Zen Buddhism's commentary on the *Laṅkāvatārasūtra*, it is stated:

> Without the *ālaya*, the cause disappears and the whole mental apparatus collapses; and when that which makes the cause operative ceases to react, the cause itself ceases to act though this does not mean its disappearance or destruction. The *manas* is the discriminating agency, but as this is possible only in the *ālaya*, on which the *manas* with all its retinue of *vijñānas* is dependent, the *manas* and the *ālaya* are in the closest possible relationship.
> – Suzuki 1999: 196

Hume's Views on Causation and Causality

The causal principle happens to be the basis for binding together the passing impressions into universal laws (Masih 2002: 322). Further, the idea of cause is derived from the relations among objects. However, according to Hume, there are three components to the idea of cause:

i. "Priority" means the cause is always prior to the effect. Causes cannot come after their effects (Searle 2004: 137).

ii. "Continuity" suggests that "the objects regarded as cause and effect are always contiguous like fire and heat" (Masih 2002: 322).

iii. "Necessary connection" means that a cause actually produces an effect. "The cause makes the effect happen, the cause necessitates the effect" (Searle 2004: 137). There is a necessary connection between cause and effect. Now the question is, "what impression produces this idea? It is not found among the known qualities of objects nor among the known relations" (Organ 1988: 54).

It seems that Hume "could not locate the impression in the objects external to the knower" (ibid.). In this context, it has, however, been observed that

> the "necessary connection"; "power", "efficacy", "force", "energy", "productive quality" and/or "agency" is located in the knower rather than in the known. – Ibid.

According to Hume,

> experience is a principle which instructs me in the several conjunctions of objects for the past. Habit is another principle which determines me to expect the same for the future. Necessary connection – the heart and core of causality – is the principle which makes up reason from cause and effect. – Ibid.: 55

It seems that Hume has tried to find out to the idea of causality through the underlying principles of cause and effect. In that he has discovered two principles: the principle of cause and the principle of causality. Both are stated as follows:

> The principle of causation says every event has a cause. The principle of causality says like causes have like effects. These, as he correctly sees, are not equivalent. For, it might be the case that every event had a cause though there was no consistency

> in what sort of effects any particular cause might have, and no consistency in what sort of causes any effect might have. And it might be the case that when there were causes and effects, like causes had like effects, even though not every event had a cause. But, says Hume, if we examine these two principles, the principle of causation and the principle of causality, we find a peculiar feature. They do not seem to be provable. They are not true by definition. That is, they are not analytic truths. So they must be synthetic empirical truths. But now, and this is the real cruncher of Hume's argument, there is no way that we could establish them by empirical methods, because any attempt to establish anything by empirical methods presupposes exactly these two principles. – Searle 2004: 138

It has, however, been observed:

> Hume's scepticism about necessary connection does not lead him to say there is no fact of the matter at all about causation. Rather, there is a fact of the matter, but it is not what we expected. We expected there to be a causal link between the cause and the effect, but what we in fact find is a sequence of events that instantiate universal laws. These two features have influenced the discussion of causation to this day. – Ibid.: 141

Some of the arguments that have been provided by Kant in justifying his objective causal principle are directed against Hume (Chatterjea et al. 2014: 222). An attempt is, therefore, made to discuss Kant's objective principle of causality.

Kant's Concept of Causality

According to Kant, "all changes take place according to the law of the connection of cause and effect" (Meiklejohn 2010-13: 149). Further, every event has a cause. It means that, "if something exists, then there must be something before it, preceding in time according to a rule" (Chatterjea et al. 2014: 208). When two events are happening in time, they are interconnected through, "a synthetical faculty of imagination, which determines the internal sense in respect of a relation in time" (Meiklejohn 2010-13: 150).

However, there are certain phenomena which exist together in the same time and the cause–effect may be simultaneous. This is explained below:

> There is heat in a room, which does not exist in the open air. I look about for the cause and find it out to be the fire. Now the fire as the cause is simultaneous with its effect, the heat in the room. In this case then, there is no succession as regards time between cause and effect, but they are simultaneous; and still the law holds good. The greater part of operating causes in nature is simultaneous with their effects; and the succession in time of the latter is produced only because the cause cannot achieve the total of its effect in one moment. But at the moment when the effect first arises, it is always simultaneous with the causality of its cause, because, if the cause had but a moment before ceased to be, the effect could not have arisen. – Meiklejohn 2010-13: 157

Action has been interpreted by Kant into two ways: (i) causality; and (ii) as substance responsible for causality. This is evident from the fact that all change is possible through a continuous action of causality (ibid.: 160). It is further stated that "Where action (consequently activity and force) exists, substance also must exist" (ibid.: 158). Action as causality is explained below:

> Every change has a cause, which evidences as its causality in the whole time during which the charge takes place. The cause, therefore, does not produce the change all at once or in one moment; but in a time, so that, as the time gradually increases from the commencing instant; *a*, to its completion at *b*, in like manner also, the quantity of the reality (*b* - *a*) is generated through the lesser degrees which are contained between the first and the last. – Ibid.: 160

Now action as substance of causality is explained:

> The conception of action indicates the relation of the subject of causality to the effect. Now because all effect consists in that which happens, therefore in the changeable, the last subject

> thereof is the permanent, as the substratum of all that changes, that is, substance. For according to the principle of causality, actions are always the first ground of all change in phenomena and, consequently, cannot be a property of a subject which itself changes, because if this were the case, other actions and another subject would be necessary to determine this change. From all this it results that action alone, as an empirical criterion is a sufficient proof of the presence of substantiality, without any necessity on my part of endeavoring to discover the permanence of substance by comparison. – Meiklejohn 2010-13: 158

Scientific Views on Causality

QUANTUM FIELD THEORY AND IMPLICATE ORDER

In the quantum field theory, the implicate order and the causal interpretation are quite simple. It is stated:

> Instead of taking a particle as the fundamental reality, start with the field. ... The field is continuous and by itself would tend to spread out from any source. However, because the super-quantum potential is non-linear and non-local, it is able under certain conditions, to provide a subtle kind of immediate connection between distant regions of the field.
>
> – Bohm and Peat 1987: 182

In the causal interpretation of field theory, ... there are two implicate orders in a specified relationship (ibid.). The first implicate order is the field itself and its movement. The second implicate is explained as follows:

> The *second implicate order* is then obtained by considering the super-quantum wave function. This is related to the whole field as the original quantum wave function is related to the particle. A more detailed treatment shows that the superquantum wave function also moves in a kind of implicate order which is, however, far subtler and more complex than the first implicate order. This then comprises the second implicate order.
>
> – Bohm and Peat: 182-83

IMPLICATE ORDER AND GENERATIVE ORDER

The relationship between the implicate order and the generative order is very close. The former is the particular case of the latter. However, explicate forms are generated in an order of unfoldment. In this process, the whole happens to be quite relevant to each part (ibid.: 184).

> If there are higher implicate orders, then a similar generative order will prevail throughout all the levels. Ultimately, it is of course, the holomovement and what may lie beyond, from which all is generated.
>
> – Ibid.

CONSCIOUSNESS AND IMPLICATE ORDER

We have dealt above mainly the material process in terms of the implicate order. "But the consciousness is much more of the implicate order than that of matter" (ibid.: 185). It may be stated that the consciousness has been captured by Bohm through the thought process, which is definitely in the implicate order.

> The very word *implicate*, meaning enfolded, suggests that one thought enfolds another and that a train of thought is actually a process of enfoldment of a succession of implications.
>
> – Ibid.

However, consciousness is organized through a generative order, which is more or less similar to the totality of the generative and implicate order that organizes matter (ibid.: 186).

INTERCONNECTION BETWEEN CONSCIOUSNESS AND MATTER

The simultaneous existence of an electron particle as well as electron wave are complementary in the quantum field theory of physics. This paves the way to find out an essential link between consciousness and the primary field. It may be noted that "the fundamental realities of the primary field and consciousness are inseparable aspects of the same underlying process" (Bhaumik 2005: 176). It has been observed:

> David Bohm has named this underlying process the *implicate order*. Basil Hiley suggests: Mind and matter are but different projections from this deeper implicate order, where such a division does not exist. He also emphasizes that "the implicate order is not some woolly metaphysical construction, it is a precise description of the underlying process", which is supported by credible mathematical analysis.
>
> – Ibid.

However, Bohm has also evolved the concept of "holomovement" with a view to capture dynamic phenomenon of which all forms of the material universe flow:

> The aim of his approach is to study the order enfolded in this holomovement, not by dealing with the structure of objects, but rather with the structure of movement, thus taking into account both the unity and the dynamic nature of the universe. According to Bohm, space and time emerge as forms flowing out of the holomovement: they too are enfolded in its order.
>
> – Capra 1989: 353

To understand the implicate order, Bohm thought that it was necessary to regard consciousness as an essential feature of the holomovement and to take it into account explicitly in his theory (ibid.). However, according to Bohm, mind and matter are interdependent and are correlated to each other, but not causally connected (ibid.).

5

Continuity

Introduction

SINCE causality is based on the notion of continuity (Woodroffe 2001: 273), an attempt has been made in this chapter to examine the essence of matter (i.e. atom and particles), *prakṛti,* consciousness and *saṁskāra* (disposition). These factors are treated as continuum, which evident from the following observations:

> The First Standard, it is true, lays down the indestructibility of the *paramāṇus,* but the Second makes *prakṛti* alone indestructible into which *tanmātras* and the rest may be reabsorbed as they are evolved out of her. The Derivatives too are persistent, if we take into consideration their patent as well as latent conditions. In the latent condition, each Derivative becomes assimilated into its immediate Root or Cause. The Third Standard asserts absolute continuity in its *Cit* working as power (*śakti*). – Ibid.: 291

The continuity of human beings takes place through *karma* (action) and its *saṁskāra* (disposition). The former leaves its impression in the mind, which is referred to as *saṁskāra.* In Indian philosophy, "*saṁskāra* covers both consciousness and unconscious tendencies of our psyche: past, present and future" (Kapani 2013: xviii). According to Sāṁkhya–Yoga, *saṁskāra* is defined as follows:

> *Saṁskāra* is a subconscious or subliminal (*sūkṣma rūpa*) continuation of what was once a conscious activity (*vyāpāra*), whether cognitive, affective or conative. A conscious activity when gone through does not absolutely end there. It simply passes into a potential and hidden (*avyakta* and *sūkṣma*) condition below the threshold of consciousness. It goes on *ad infinitum*

> more and more below the level of the ordinary consciousness. This for pragmatic reasons lights up only between certain limits. Stimuli and brain excitements of certain degrees of intensity only evoke response. But the activities do not leave when pragmatic consciousness fails to notice them. They go on. Thus, the course of any activity (*vyāpāra*) in mental life displays itself when above the threshold of consciousness as conscious activity and when it sinks below the threshold it is called *saṁskāra* or tendency or potential due to unconscious mental operations (Woodroffe 2001: 105). In this sense, the mental life is now recognized as a continuum.

It may, however, be stated that the mind at the time of birth is not a *tabula rasa*, but it is a storehouse of predispositions. Therefore, according to Vedānta, man is born with his inherent *saṁskāras* (ibid.: 107).

Matter as Atom and Particles

The scientific views on matter in terms of atoms, energy, etc. are dealt within physics. Although these qualities of scientific matter are quite important for human life, they are not objects of our perception. The main reason for not perceiving the scientific matter by human beings is that the scientists have reached to the rock bottom of matter. It is, therefore, stated that

> all matter consisted of atoms and all atoms consisted of protons, neutrons and electrons. These so-called elementary particles were seen as ultimate indestructible units of matter: atoms in the Democritean sense. – Capra 1989: 85

According to Democritus (460–360 BCE), "the material atoms alone can account for the whole universe" (Masih 2002: 3).

It is, however, observed that with the discovery of three subatomic particles, it was realized that atom was not the main cause of the universe as stated by Democritus.

> Atom is made of still smaller particles. These micro particles are the electron, the proton and the neutron. The neutron is slightly

> heavier than the proton. For practical purposes, the neutron and the proton may be considered to have equal weights. But the electron is much lighter, 1836 times lighter than the proton.
>
> – Panda 2008: 24

Atom, "consists of a positively charged nucleus in which protons and neutrons are bound together, balanced by the negatively charged electrons surrounding it" (Bhaumik 2005: 128). This means:

> As particle and anti-particle unite to liberate energy, so also, if enough energy is available, particles and anti-particles can be created out of pure energy in the reverse process of annihilation.
>
> – Panda 2008: 28

There is no single particle which can be the building unit of universe. This is mainly because several particles appear and disappear. In fact, matter is a packet of energy. In this context it is stated that

> matter is energy and vice versa. Again, energy is both wave and corpuscular, continuous and discrete. The substratum of energy is field which is unmanifested to our senses. Field gets manifested either as energy or as matter particles. There is unified field which is the canvas on which energy and matter appear as paintings. – Ibid.: 54

The energy as basis of universe will be discussed in detail later. Here we would like to state that the particles which constitute atom and energy are continuum.

Complementarity in Duality of Matter

At the atomic level, there is a duality in matter; it appears both as particles and waves. However, in some situations, particle aspect becomes dominant, while in others particles behave like waves. This dual aspect is also exhibited by light and all electromagnetic radiation (Capra 1989: 164).

> When these particles of light travel through space they appear as vibrating electric and magnetic fields, which show all the characteristic behaviour of waves. Electrons are normally

> considered to be particles and yet when a beam of these particles is sent through a small slit, it is diffracted just like a beam of light, in other words electrons too behave like the waves.
> – Capra 1989: 164

In quantum theory, however, it is not possible to speak of the particle's trajectory

> when we say that the particle is also wave. What we mean is that the wave pattern as a whole is manifestation of the particle. The picture of travelling waves is thus totally different from that of travelling particles. – Ibid.: 165

It may further be stated that in quantum theory the atomic phenomena can be described in terms of probabilities. Therefore, it can never be said that atomic particles exist at certain place nor it can be said that it does not exist.

> Being a probability pattern, the particle has tendencies to exist in various places and thus manifests a strange kind of physical reality between existence and non-existence. We cannot, therefore, describe the state of the particle in terms of fixed opposite concepts. – Ibid.: 166

The duality of the particle has been resolved through the probability waves in the sense that the pair of opposites is transcended by the atomic reality (Capra 1989: 166). Yet, it is most difficult to accept this transcended theory of quantum physics (ibid.: 167). This duality has, however, been reconciled in another way. It is stated:

> A photon or an electron has dual aspect: a wave aspect and a particle aspect. Two aspects are complementary. The one aspect excludes the other aspect. That is why the two aspects are not contradictory. A contradiction between them could arise only if the two aspects could be observed at the same time. But this never happens and we have compelling theoretical arguments that this could not happen. *The wave and the particle aspects are complementary and not contradictory* (emphasize added by italics).
> – Kothari 2002: 311

It has been further explained:

> At the root of the wave–particle duality is *the principle of absolute indistinguishability, absolute identities of particles of the same kind.* All electrons in the universe are absolutely identical, absolutely indistinguishable from one another. – Kothari 2002: 313

In the total wave function, the identity of individual electron is completely lost. There is no separate individuality of electron in the total wave function. This is explained as follows:

> *The electrons have submerged themselves, as it were in one "brotherhood" of electrons.* The Many have become One ... when we speak of the total-wave-function or the field, and the many identical particles incorporated in the wave function, it is not sort of an aggregate, a sum of the Many. In an aggregate, the Oneness is no more than an euphemism for the Many that are still visible, may be dimly in the aggregate. The concept of Oneness in quantum mechanics is a totally, fundamentally, new concept. ... The One is an abstract space, the Many in physical space. The two aspects are complementary (emphasis added by italics).
>
> – Ibid.: 314

Energy as Basis of Universe

When one penetrates deeper into the matter, one may find two things:

i. the wave and the particle aspects are complementary and not contradictory; and
ii. here is unity in the sense that the universe arises from a common source and things are interconnected.

Some of these issues are discussed below.

The following observation of James Jeans regarding waves may be noted:

> The tendency of modern physics is to resolve the whole material universe into waves, and nothing but waves. These waves are of

> two kinds: bottled up waves which we call matter, and unbottled waves which we call radiation or light. The process of annihilation of matter is merely that of unbottling imprisoned wave energy and setting it free to travel through space. These concepts reduce the whole universe to a world of radiation, potential or existent and it no longer seems surprising that the fundamental particles, of which matter is built up, should exhibit many of properties of waves. – Quoted in Taimni 1987a: 107

Dematerialization of matter may be supported on the basis of experiment conducted by Michael Faraday and James Clark Maxwell. It has been observed:

> Each charge creates a "disturbance" or a "condition" in the space around it so that other charge, when it is present feels a force. This condition in space which has the potential producing a force called a field. ... This was a most profound change in our conception of physical reality. ... Now the force concept was replaced by the much subtler concept of a field which had its own reality and could be studied without any reference to material bodies. – Capra 1989: 68

Further, the concepts of time and space, based on the theory of relativity, have modified not only the whole framework to describe nature but also realization that mass is nothing but a form of energy as well.

> Even an object at rest has energy stored up in its mass, and the relation between the two is given by the famous equation $E = mc^2$, c being the speed of light. – Ibid.: 72

This formula had led to the discovery of atomic energy. It has not only revolutionized the fundamental conceptions of science but brought about for reaching changes in our life (Taimni 2005: 226).

It is stated:

> All the matter that makes up our everyday world is composed of two kinds of fundamental particles: quarks and electrons.
> – Bhaumik 2005: 128

According to Einstein, quarks and other elementary particles are, however, nothing but discrete packets of energy (Bhaumik 2005: 128).

Now a question arises:

> If everything is ultimately made of one substance – energy – does the nature provide so many different types of fields of energy to work its magic? Most physicists are now quite convinced that these diverse fields including a few that Einstein has not considered are nothing but different aspects of a single field.
>
> – Ibid.: 139

This shows that all the fields in our universe arise from a common source which is called the primary field (ibid.: 146).

However, there are two kinds of energy: potential and kinetic. In the former, there is no movement and it is based on force. Whereas, the latter is based on motion or movement. Further, in the case of kinetic energy also two kinds of energy are involved:

i. vibrational as in the case of radiation; and

ii. molecular as in the case of motion of atoms and molecules.

Both are interrelated and interchangeable. This can be seen from the fact:

> Vibrational energy of radiation can set molecules and atoms in motion as happens when sunlight falls on physical objects and they get heated. – Taimni 1987b: 116-17

It has been further observed that in the duality of matter and energy, the energy happens to be the basic element. Whereas, the matter is derived from the condensation of energy (ibid.: 117).

The most peculiar thing about energy is that without energy no activities could get started. Yet, even physicists do not know what exactly energy is. However,

> it reveals itself to us through the forms it takes. We can measure the surge through an electrical circuit or observe the explosion

> that results from a chemical reaction; we can feel the heat of energy of the sun's nuclear alchemy or thrill to the kinetic energy of *g* – forces produced by a roller coaster. – Bhaumik 2005: 129

This shows that it is only energy that works in different kinds of activities.

The other important thing about energy is that the net energy of the universe happens to be zero. Therefore, one may infer that the universe might have started from zero (ibid.: 195). It may, therefore, be said that the creation of the universe itself seems to have started from this mystical number of zero.

> Zero appears as vanishing point between positive and negative infinities. In other words, once we include negative numbers, could zero as easily stand for the source of everything as the realm of nothing? – Ibid.: 196

The Big Bang itself supports the idea that the universe is thought to have had zero size (Hawking 1988: 117).

What is the source from which this energy came? The answer to this question may be seen in the following observation:

> The total energy of the universe is exactly zero. The matter in the universe is made of the positive energy. However, the matter is all attracting itself by gravity. Two pieces of matter that are close to each other have less energy than the same two pieces a long way apart, because you have to expand energy to separate them against the gravitational force that is pulling them together. Thus, in a sense the gravitational field has negative energy. In the case of universe that is approximately uniform in space, one can show that this negative gravitational energy exactly cancels the positive energy represented by the matter. So the total energy of the universe is zero. – Ibid.: 129

Prakr̥ti

Prakr̥ti is known as *avyakta*, the unmanifested and undifferentiated state. The same thing may be said in another way:

> *Prakṛti* is the state in which all its constituent elements are in absolute equilibrium. – Acharya 1985: 134

In that, *prakṛti* becomes as the symbol of harmony: "The root of the universe therefore is perfect harmony" (ibid.). However, creation begins with the disturbance in the elements which constitute *prakṛti*. It is uncaused. This is evident from the following verse:

> मूले मूलभावादमूलं मूलम्।
> *mūle mūlabhāvādamulaṁ mūlam* ।
>
> Since the root has no root, the root is rootless.
> – Sinha 2013: 111

According to the *Vṛtti:*

> There being no root, that is no cause, of *mūla-prakṛti* (the Root Evolvent), the cause which is rootless, is the root (of all). The same is *prakṛti*. – Ibid.

The above verse is further explained as follows:

> Now in order to establish that she is the cause of all, the eternity of *prakṛti* is being established, for the purpose of proving that *Puruṣa* is *kūṭastha* (immutable) in all circumstances. The root material cause of the twenty-three principles,[1] that is, *pradhāna,* is rootless, because a further root cannot be possible, as in that case, there would be an infinite regression. Such is the meaning.
> – Ibid.

Prakṛti is just opposite to *Puruṣa,* because the former is involved in the causality, whereas the latter undergoes no transformation. However, *prakṛti* and *Puruṣa* both are eternal (ibid.: 119). Further, *prakṛti* is unborn (Ram 1995: 85).

---

1 It may be noted that there are twenty-five principles of Sāṁkhya system of philosophy. These are: five *tanmātras*; five organs of perception; five organs of action; five primordial elements; one *puruṣa*; one *prakṛti*; one *mahān* (*mahat*); one *ahaṁkāra*; and one mind. See Tilak 2000: 249.

It has also been stated that *prakṛti* is all-pervading, because what is limited cannot be the material cause of all things (Sinha 2013: 120). *Prakṛti* does not merge into anything else, it is the pure unmanifest state of all products (Swami Virupakshananda 2003: 52).

GUṆA

It may be stated that the concept of *guṇas* is embodied in the modern scientific conception of the construction of atom. In this context, it is stated:

> In this scientific conception of the atom has the proton, the electron and the neutron. These three are, in a sense, comparable to the concept of the Sāṁkhya of the *sattva, rajas* and *tamas* respectively. The proton provides the coalescence or the form of the atom, the electron gives us energy and the neutron provides mass. The Sāṁkhya felt that the atom would exhibit the characteristics of the *guṇa* which predominate in it.
>
> – Catalina 1968: 32-33

Sattva is intelligent stuff or potential consciousness (ibid.). It is also referred to as light and illumination. In terms of colour it is treated as white. *Rajas* is energy stuff and involves in action. It is of red colour. *Tamas* is mass stuff and affects more gross matter, inorganic matter. It indicates darkness and has restraining capacity. However, these *guṇas* are mutually dominating, supporting, proactive and cooperative.

Mutually Dominating

When one becomes active for some purpose, it dominates over other. For instance,

> *Sattva* attains its calm nature only after dominating over (or subjugating), the *rajas* and *tamas* attributes. Similarly, the *rajas* attains its agitated nature by subduing the *sattva* and *tamas* attributes and *tamas* attains to its torpid condition by subjugating both *sattva* and *rajas*. – Swami Virupakshananda 2003: 43-44

Mutually Supporting

Sattva, resting upon activity and restraint, subserves *rajas* and *tamas* attributes with illumination. *Rajas*, resting upon illumination and restraint, subserves *sattva* and *tamas* with activity; and *tamas*, resting on illumination and activity, subserves *sattva* and *rajas* with restraint (Swami Virupakshananda 2003: 44).

Mutually Productive

It is stated that one produces its effects resting upon the other two. Production here means modification and it is always of the same nature as of the attributes (ibid.).

Mutually Cooperative

They are mutually concomitants and never exist separately from one another (ibid.).

Consciousness

Consciousness is the ultimate principle capable of explaining everything in the universe. The most important feature of consciousness is that it has the capacity to transcend the limitations of time and space.

> Everything physical is bound by space and time or indeed by the space–time continuum. This is so because continuum itself is responsible for their coming into being. – Singh 2004: 68-69

This is further explained as follows:

> It is owing to its transcendence of the space–time continuum that there is the possibility of such a colossal variation in the range of consciousness as underlies the ideas of transcendence, individuality and universality associated with it. *Brahman, Ātman* and the universe are respective representatives of the three ranges. It is a matter of common knowledge now that all these three ranges have been found out by Upaniṣadic sages as equivalent to one another. This is manifest in the great

> statements "I am *Brahman*" and "All this verily is *Brahman*". While the first one of these statements bears out the equivalence of the Transcendent with the individual, the second one does the same in regard to the Transcendent and the universal. Had consciousness not been free of the limitations of space and time, the universal could not be declared as equivalent to the individual and much less could the Transcendent have been realized as such in relationship to the universal and the individual. ... In fact, the Transcendent itself uses the continuum as a total of becoming other than Itself. – Singh 2004: 69

The Buddhist also holds the continuum of consciousness. This is stated below:

> The life of consciousness to be a beginningless, never-ending continuum in which each precedent conscious moment is followed by a subsequent conscious moment, which derives its existence from the former and goes on producing its duplicates without end. Thus, so far consciousness *qua* consciousness is concerned, it is an eternal, timeless process without a definite beginning or an abrupt end. – Mookerjee 1993: 205

The Concept of Saṁskāra in Sāṁkhya-Yoga

In *Sāṁkhya-Kārikā* 52 it is stated:

> Without the (subjective) dispositions, there would be no (objective) evolution of the *tanmātras*; and without the objective, there would be no subjective. Therefore, there proceeds a twofold evolution, known as the objective and the subjective.
> – Swami Virupakshananda 2003: 107-08

This shows in the subjective evolution, the dispositions (*vāsanās*) are inherent; and it influences the perception in the phenomenal world. This has been clarified in the commentary of *Yogasūtra* IV.6 of Patañjali. It states:

> The "natural mind" is the product of evolutionary growth and is the repository of the *saṁskāras* of all the experiences which it has throughout during the course of successive lives. These

> *saṁskāras* in their totality are referred to as *karmāśaya*, the vehicle of *karmas*.
>
> – Taimni 1999: 391

It is thus evident that the concepts of *saṁskāra* and *vṛtti* are introduced in perception by Patañjali, the author of the *Yogasūtra*. *Vṛtti* is derived from the root *vṛt* which means to exist. This is explained below:

> So *vṛtti* is a way of existing. In considering the ways in which a thing exists, we may consider its modifications, states, activities or its functions. All these connotations are present in the meaning of *vṛtti* but in the present context, this word is best translated by the words modifications or functionings. ... Since *citta* has a functional existence and comes into being only when consciousness is affected by matter, the word functionings perhaps expresses to the maximum degree the significance of *vṛtti* in the present context.
>
> – Ibid.: 8

Vṛttis are fivefold: right knowledge (*pramāṇa*), wrong knowledge (*viparyāya*), fancy (*vikalpa*), sleep (*nidrā*) and memory (*smṛti*). Right knowledge and wrong knowledge are those images which are formed by the direct contact through the sense organs with the objects, whereas *vikalpa* and *smṛti* comprise all those images which are formed without any direct contact with the objects. However, in the dream state, there is no control over such images, but is mostly influenced by the desires present in the subconscious mind (ibid.: 14).

It may, however, be stated that the moment consciousness comes in contact with matter, it starts exerting human life. Thereafter *saṁskāras* (dispositions) begin to form. As evolution progresses, dispositions become more complicated due to desires and actions. These actions leave some kind of impression, which restricts us in some way later.

> Our desires produce potential energy which draws us irresistibly to the environment or conditions in which they can be satisfied.
>
> – Ibid.: 394

Our thoughts also produce *saṁskāras* (Taimni 1999: 395).

In fact, the doctrine of *saṁskāra* is directly related to the law of *karma*. This may be seen from the following observation:

> The subconscious impressions can be traced to the residual *karma* of the past lives which accompanies *jīva* from birth to birth in two forms: (1) the individual tendencies, propensities, interests and urges called *vāsanā*, and (2) the merit and de-merit of the past actions. These accompany the soul after death, remain in seed form and bear fruit in the coming life in accordance with the law of *karma*. The *vāsanā* propels him to act in a particular direction, and merit and demerit (*dharma-adharma*) fructifies at proper occasions causing pleasant or unpleasant incidents of life. The seat of the *saṁskāras* according to Yoga is *karmāśaya*.
>
> – Safaya 1976: 276-77

However, there seems to be cyclic causation between *saṁskāra* and *vṛtti*. The former causes the latter, which in turn leaves some impressions to be accumulated in the previous *saṁskāras* (ibid.: 277).

In the *vṛtti* theory, the mind gets modified according to the impression created by the object. In such a situation, the mind at times obscures consciousness (Taimni 1999: 395). Therefore, it may not be possible,

> to obtain a true impression of the object as long as the mind itself is not free from its *vṛttis*. The impression created will depend upon the condition of receiving mind and as all minds are in different conditions because they have followed different paths in their evolution, they must get different impressions from the same object. – Ibid.: 411

It may be noted that mind becomes one with object only in *samādhi* when all the *vṛttis* are suppressed.

However, according to Sāṁkhya, "a *saṁskāra* is tendency, while a *vṛtti* is action: both are *vyāpāra* (energizing) of *antaḥkaraṇa*" (Woodroffe 2001: 121). There is no denying the fact that

> an external world actually existing outside along with its objects, but all this comes to be known to us in the forms *antaḥkaraṇa* takes by projecting itself on the same via the senses. – Singh 2004: 75

In the above-mentioned *Sāṁkhya-Kārikā* 52, there is a defect of mutual dependence. This problem has been solved by Vācaspati Miśra in the following commentary:

> Experience is not possible without the vehicles of experience in the form of sense organs: and the creation of internal organs in turn is not possible without the dispositions such as virtue and the rest. Nor Discriminating Wisdom, which brings about the emancipation, is possible without both of these evolutions. Thus is established the appropriateness of both forms of Evolution (viz. subjective evolution proceeding from the *buddhi* and the objective evolution proceeding from the *tanmātras*). The defect of mutual dependence (*anyonyāśraya doṣa*) does not affect this theory, because the creation being eternal, it would be like the analogy of the seed and the sprout (*bījāṅkura-nyāya*, which is a maxim involving an eternal series of seed and sprout. As the seed produces the sprout, so the latter in turn reproduces the former. Each, therefore, is a cause and an effect). The production of subjective and objective evolutions even at the very beginning of the present cycle (*kalpa*) is due to the subliminal impressions left behind by the corresponding subjective and objective evolutions in the earlier cycle: thus, this theory of the emanations of the evolutions is quite appropriate and is accepted by all.
>
> – Swami Virupakshananda 2003: 108-09

Advaita Vedānta Theory of Saṁskāra (Disposition)

According to Vedānta, each cognition lasts as long as the corresponding mental mode lasts.

> When the mode disappears it leaves an impression (*saṁskāra*) on the mind. The memory of cognition is due to this. A cognitive mode does not require any other cognitive mode for its manifestation, so it is said to be self-manifest.
>
> – Swami Satprakashananda 2001a: 94

In fact, the cumulative effect of *saṁskāras* determines an individual's course of life here and hereafter, indicating thereby the continuity of human beings. It may be noted that the subtle impressions (*saṁskāras*) left

> by *karma* on the mind of doer that cling to him whatever he may be, here or beyond, fructify in due course. As a man sows, so does he reap. – Swami Satprakashananda 2001a: 210

While commenting on the basis of *Chāndogya Upaniṣad* V.10.5, it is stated:

> In the case of tendencies, there is no total destruction of results of work, and hence there is the possibility for residual results. Since this is so, therefore, it is logical that transmigration becomes possible owing to the results remaining as residue after the enjoyment of (other) results of actions.
>
> – Swami Gambhirananda 2003: 366

This shows that human beings perpetuate their rebirth in *saṁsāra* (empirical world) because of the residue of kārmic forces which reside in *antaḥkaraṇa* (mind) as *saṁskāra.* However, the former experience has been explained on the basis of commentary on *Bṛhadāraṇyaka Upaniṣad* IV.4.2. This passage shows that how every organ gets unified with the subtle body of the dying man.

> When the vital force departs, all the organs follow. Then the self has particular consciousness, and goes to the body which is related to the consciousness. It is followed by knowledge, work and past experience. – Swami Madhavananda 1997: 489, v. IV.4.3

The commentary on this verse summarized below is worth noting:

> As a matter of fact, everybody has at that moment a consciousness which consists of impressions in the form of particular modifications of his mind (regarding the next life). ... It has been stated that departing self, loaded with materials, goes making noises like a cart. (This load consists of) the impressions of experiences regarding the results of past actions. These impressions take part in initiating fresh actions as also in bringing

> past actions to fruition; hence they too accompany. Without these impressions no action can be done, nor any results of past actions be achieved, for the organs are not skilful in unpractised work. But when the organs are promoted to work by the impressions of past experience, they can easily attain skill even without practice in this life. It is frequently observed that some are clever in certain kinds of work, such as painting, from their very birth, even without practice in this life, while others are unskilful even in some very easy tasks. ... Hence, these three – knowledge, work and past experience – are the food on the way to the next world, corresponding to the load of the carter. Since these three are the means of attaining another body and enjoying (the results of one's past work), therefore one should cultivate only the good forms of them, so that one may have a desirable body and desirable enjoyments. This is the purport of the whole passage. ... Therefore, the impressions called past experience, under the control of person's knowledge and work, stretch out, like a leech, from the body, retaining their seat in the heart, as in the dream state, and build another body in accordance with his past work; they leave their seat, the old body, when a new body is made.
>
> – Swami Madhavananda 1997: 491-93

However, relationship between *saṁskāra* and *saṁsāra* may be established by the fact that

> after the actions are exhausted, the soul returns together with (the residual) *karma*, as is known from the Upaniṣads and Smṛtis along the path followed (by it) while going as also differently.
>
> – Swami Gambhirananda 2000: 565, v. III.1.8

This is based on *Brahmasūtra-Bhāṣya* III.1.8. The commentary on this *sūtra* is summarized below:

> There is a direct Vedic text revealing the descent of the souls along with their (residual) *karma*. ... Smṛti also shows that the souls descend with (residual) *karma*. ... Since the Upaniṣads mention that all results of actions are eradicated on the dawn of enlightement, ... the conclusion remains intact that the souls descend with their *karmas*. And when they come down, they

> do so along the path followed (by them) while going up, as also differently. *Yathetam* (lit. as it had been reached) means – "just as they had gone", and *anevam* means "in the opposite manner".
> – Swami Gambhirananda 2000: 567-71

The Concept of Saṁskāra in the Philosophy of Bauddha Dharma

Saṁskāra is referred to as *saṅkhāra* in Buddhism. It is

> compounded of the prefix *saṁ* meaning "with" or "together with" and a form of the verbal root *kr̥* (to do or make). *Saṁskāra* literally means "put or to make together" or simply "formation".
> – Waldron 2003: 23

In this context, it is stated:

> *Saṅkhāras* to act is to make, and it is by virtue of making or putting together that *saṅkhāra* becomes active. ... *sāṅkhāras* both make and are made. The term *saṅkhāra* includes in its meaning both effective action and the effects of action. – Devdas 2008: 121

It may, however, be noted that in view of the conditioned origination (i.e. *pratītya-samutpāda*), it is observed that

> *saṅkhāras* serve as the link between past experience and future goals. They preserve the continuity with past conditions, although this continuity is not simple and straightforward, but marked by complex relationship between networks of causes and conditions. – Ibid.: 163-64

It is further stated:

> The conditioning and conditioned processes that constitute *saṅkhāras* are also "carriers" of kārmic merit and demerit, through them complex networks of causes are formed, linking the time when an act is performed and the time when the consequences of the act are experienced. – Ibid.: 164

The above observation has been reassured by the other statement that

> the kārmic formations, the *saṅkhāra* serve to perpetuate the cycle in two ways in the series of dependent arising: they constitute both the basis for sāṁsāric continuity as well as the causes of perpetuating the cycle. These twin roles are implicit in the process-product nature of the concept of *saṁskāra* itself.
>
> – Waldron 2003: 23

This process-product nature is used "to refer both to the process (or more accurately, activity) ... and to the product of that activity" (ibid.: 191).

The fact, however, remains that in the psychological sense,

> *saṅkhāra* refers more narrowly to the volitions, dispositions, and actions that constitute human activities, insofar as these are both constructed complexes formed from past actions, as well as constructive and formative influences conditioning present and future actions. – Ibid.: 23

This seems to be contradictory because both "a cause and result at the same time to be both constructed and constructing" (ibid.). Yet, it has been observed:

> Two properties are simultaneously found in many processes especially those of living organisms, which develop and perpetuate themselves through their own interactive feedback processes embodied in patterns of circular causality as is now widely understood in the natural sciences. – Ibid.

Now let us see how the kārmic forces turn into *saṁskāra* in the framework of dependent origination.

DEPENDENT ORIGINATION AND SAṀSKĀRA

Dependent origination is essentially meant to take

> an account of the causal structure of the round of existence (*vaṭṭa*), disclosing the conditions that sustain the wheel of birth and death and make it revolve from one existence to another.
>
> – Bhikkhu Bodhi 1999: 295

Under such a system, dependent on ignorance arise the kārmic formations (*saṁskāras*). Further, depending on kārmic formations arises consciousness. However,

> when the mental continuum of a living being is imbued with ignorance, then his volitional activity generates *kamma* with potency to produce results in the future.
>
> – Bhikkhu Bodhi 1999: 295

It has been concluded that *saṅkhāras*

> have a major role in forming the person, who is conceived as the agent of action. *Saṅkhāras* also produce the purposive acts of body, speech and mind through which the person develops and finds self-expression within the processes of *kamma* and rebirth.
>
> – Devdas 2008: 163

Saṁskāras are volitional in nature. Therefore, *cetanā* and *saṁskāra* are the same (Haldar 2001: 77). It may be noted:

> *Saṁskāras* are recognized as an important instrument for constitution: *cetanā* or volition is described as the first stirring of consciousness. – Ibid.: 75

However, "*saṁskāra* forms a link (dynamic continuity) between the two different births" (ibid.: 74).

SAṀSKĀRA (KĀRMIC FORMATIONS) AND VIÑÑĀNA (CONSCIOUSNESS)

In the dependent origination, the kārmic formations (*saṁskāras*) condition the arising of consciousness or cognitive awareness (Waldron 2003: 14). However, consciousness is

> a precondition not only for the development of a new sentient body (name and form) in this life but also for the growth of kārmic formations. – Ibid.: 21

This may be explained as follows:

> This last moment of consciousness before death is known as the *cuti-viññāṇa*. Immediately on its cessation, contingent upon some *kamma* conditioned by the *cuti-viññāṇa* and driven by craving and

> ignorance not yet abanded, there arises in the mother's womb the first stirring of consciousness of the succeeding birth. It is known as the rebirth-linking consciousness (*paṭisandhi-viññāṇa*). Not being carried over from the previous life, this rebirth-linking consciousness newly arises at the precise moment of conception. In other words, no transmigration of consciousness is being posited here, but rather a causally linked stream (*sota*) of discrete moments of consciousness. – Mcdermott 1999: 169

The above observations indicate that *saṁskāra*s (kārmic forces) and consciousness play an important role in the continuity of human beings.

David Bohm's Views on Consciousness and Matter

According to Bohm,

> matter and consciousness are manifestations of implicate order, which enfolds all that which is. We may remark that this is strikingly similar to the Vedāntic notion, in light of which contradiction between mind and body is resolved. – Joshi 2006: 26

In casual interpretation of the field theory, there are two implicate orders: the first implicate order is the field itself and the second implicate order is obtained by the super-quantum wave function (Bohm and Peat 1987: 182). However, in an order of unfoldment, it is mentioned:

> If there are higher implicate orders, then a similar generative order will prevail throughout all the levels. Ultimately, it is, of course, the holomovement, and what may lie beyond, from which all is generated. – Ibid.: 184

The concept of implicate order has, however, been compared with Sāṁkhya–Yoga's concept of *mūla-prakṛti* or *citta* that is an unmanifest (*avyakta*), yet determinative implicate order which is constantly generating the explicate order or in other words the manifest (*vyakta*) world of ordinary awareness (Larson 2003: 186). Against this manifestation, there is pure contentless consciousness

(*Puruṣa*), being the essential witness (*sākṣī*) whose simple presence "allows everything to be, and like the hologram it is present in its entirety in every self-awareness (hence *Puruṣa bahutva*)" (Larson 2003: 187).

According to Bohm and Peat, consciousness happens to partake much more of the implicate order than that of matter (1987: 185). Consciousness is captured by the thought process which is definitely the implicate order. The word implicate means enfolded. It suggests that one thought enfolds another (ibid.). However, the main approach adopted by Bohm and Peat (ibid.: 211-12) regarding consciousness is given below:

i. Consciousness has two aspects: (a) material, and (b) mental. The material aspect can be studied scientifically. But the mental aspect would be rather difficult to capture by scientific studies. Therefore, one has to go beyond the usual approaches in which the mind and the matter are two separate but interacting streams.

ii. The root of the manifestation lies in the ultimate depths of the implicate and generative orders of the totality of matter, life and mind. In this context, it has been observed that "*even inanimate matter must have some kind of mental aspect*" (emphasis added by italics).

iii. There is no absolutely sharp "cut" or break between consciousness, life and matter, whether animate or inanimate. Therefore, it has been concluded that as the consciousness approached to its origin of generative order, the mental aspect becomes more important, "while in the journey of 'downstream', the manifest physical side becomes more evident".

Now the question arises of how the mental side of consciousness is related to the material side of the consciousness. The relationship between both aspects is tried to be established through awareness and attention.

AWARENESS AND ATTENTION

Consciousness has been treated as the total state of "knowingness" of the individual. Therefore, the term "conscious awareness" is taken to mean a consciousness (i.e. a knowingness). It is also stated that consciousness is only a small part of the total field of consciousness or knowingness (Bohm and Peat 1987: 214). Whereas,

> the word attention means literally stretching the mind toward something. This implies an inner activity that is needed to grasp the object of interest mentally. Even physically it has been demonstrated that a kind of attention must operate, as for example, in the eye's scanning pattern, which varies according to each person's concept of the object that is being looked at.
>
> – Ibid.: 214-15

In this context, it has been stated that the movement of attention along with the sensitivity of awareness is constantly bringing the content of physical side to the "mental" side. In this way, a relationship between the physical side and the mental side has been established in consciousness. However, in the context of an interconnection between consciousness and matter, Bohm has stated that like mind and matter, both are interdependent and correlated to each other, but not causally connected (Capra 1989: 353).

Implications of Main Tendencies of Self-Consciousness for Human Life

The main tendencies of self-consciousness are self-protection, self-procreation, disembodied survival with the mental, self-realization and immorality. These are discussed below.

SELF-PROTECTION

Pure consciousness manifests through the mind which creates the duality of subjective and objective in experiencing the physical world. In this process, the main feature of consciousness being the self-concentricity (pure consciousness) is reversed, in the sense that it gets mainly involved in the objective side in experiencing the world affairs. In that, the consciousness has to become other than the itself. This attitude of outer orientation towards everything other than of itself, generates fear, which in turn results into the tendency of self-protection (Singh 2004: 217).

INSTINCT OF SELF-PROCREATION

The instinct of procreation according to the Vedic vision is stated in the following lines:

> It traces the inclination of the humans to sex back to the creativity of consciousness itself as represented in its concentricity of *Ātman* as also in its extensity of *Brahman*. *Ātman* alone was there in the beginning, observes the Upaniṣad and continues to state that, on account of not feeling enjoyable its loneliness, it divided itself into two, the man and the woman. As man and woman are just two parts of one and the same integral being, points out the Upaniṣad, they naturally feel attracted to each other and find their greatest fulfilment in embracing each other. This is how, observes the Upaniṣad, the humans were born. – Ibid.: 218

It is further observed:

> When the Upaniṣad notes that the organ of generation is the object of all enjoyments uniformally, it amounts simply to suggest that the joy generated by the act of sex is the highest on the instinctive level, as it results in tracing back, in its own way, to the original state of the unity of consciousness. – Ibid.

DISEMBODIED SURVIVAL OF THE MENTAL AND CONSCIOUSNESS

The embodied self, at death, departs

> with subtle body all its components, i.e. the five *prāṇas* (the five phases of the vital principle), the five organs of perception, the five motor organs and the mind (*antaḥkaraṇa*) go with him.
> – Swami Satprakashananda 1974: 176

In other words, the subtle body (including its components) is immortal (Radhakrishnan 2009: 683).[2]

The word subtle at first sight seems to suggest that "consciousness is some form of disembodied spirit" (Bohm and Peat 1987: 211). However,

> the doctrine of transmigration is based on the eternity of consciousness. As consciousness can neither originate nor end, so its existence throughout the past must be conceived as repeated embodiment like the present birth.
>
> – Swami Swahananda 2001: 133, v. VI.23

The argument for reincarnation has been stated in a different way by Indian philosophy. This is given below:

> The new born child's sucking reflex which enables it to suck its mother's breast is due to the revival of its impressions of the experience of gratifying its hunger by sucking its mother's breast which the child must have had in its previous birth. This is a stock argument for reincarnation adduced by Indian philosophers. A modern thinker would not attach much importance to this argument, although he cannot explain satisfactorily the purpose and well-directed character of certain basic bodily reflexes. They are absolutely essential for self-preservation and they are directly aimed at fulfilling some important physiological need. How did the body acquire the habit of acting according to the reflex? Feeling hungry is intrinsic to the living body but a particular type of activity cannot also be regarded as intrinsic to the living body. The sucking reflex cannot be regarded similar to the involuntary movement of a limb of the body to avoid fire or any other object causing some unpleasant sensation. The sucking reflex has a special character. It is not thrusting the mouth towards the breast. It is holding the best nipple in the mouth and pressing it in certain way. This is just like a learned activity but is not at all learned. There is some inner urge which prompts the child to pucker its lips so that they can suck milk from the breast. This

[2] This is based on *Muṇḍaka Upaniṣad* II.2.2.

> urge is equated with pre-natal impressions or what are called *saṁskāras* by Indian philosophers. – Dravid 1995: 571-72

The above observations may be supported from different sources of Buddhism. These are stated below.

Consciousness as Transmigration and Buddhist Soul

TRANSMIGRATION OF CONSCIOUSNESS

In the *Mahāratnakūṭasūtra*, it is clearly stated that

> the consciousness is reincarnated together with the *prāṇa* element and the elements of subtle memory, feeling and *dharmas*.
> – Chang 1983: 227

The following observations of this *sūtra* are also worth noting:

i. Sentient beings who are subject to transmigration have awareness. Because they have awareness, they have feelings, and as a result, the consciousness takes on different bodies together with good and evil *karmas* (ibid.: 229).
ii. When the sentient being's life comes to an end, his body dies, the consciousness will leave his body to take birth again together with his *karmas* (ibid.: 231).

The above observations indicate that it is the same consciousness along with his *karma* is reborn in the human beings.

BUDDHIST SOUL

According to the Tibetan Buddhism, the Buddhist soul is defined as follows:

> The extremely subtle body is called the indestructible drop: it is a tiny energy pattern existing normally only in the centre of the heart wheel or complex. The extremely subtle mind that corresponds to it is the intuition of clear light, called transparency. At this extremely subtle level, the body–mind distinction is abandoned, as the two are virtually inseparable. This indestructible-drop transparent awareness is the Buddhist

> soul, the deepest seat of life and awareness, whose continuity is indestructible, though it constantly changes while moving from life to life. To achieve conscious identification with this body-mind, to experience reality from this extremely subtle level of awareness, is tantamount to attaining Buddhahood.
>
> – Robert 2001: 36

It is further stated that "this extremely subtle indestructible drop is very similar to the Hindu notion of the self (*Ātman*) or Supreme Self (*Paramātman*), which reached as the absolute negation of all petty, individual personality selves".

The above concept of transmigration of consciousness may be further supported by the fact that the impression of experience generated by *karmas* of human beings of earlier births are recorded in the *karmāśaya*.

By reaching the stage of pure consciousness, one experiences *Nirvāṇa*, breaking the cycle of rebirth: one also sees his previous rebirths, which have been recorded in the *karmāśaya* of human being.

Epilogue

In this study two things are involved: the evolutionary universe (*brahmāṇḍa*) and self-conscious human being (*piṇḍa*). The former is "out there" and the latter is "out here". If latter does not exist, it is indeed difficult to know or perceive "out there". This is mainly because "out here" has the mind through which "out there" is known. Whether "out there" has mind or not, it is, indeed, difficult to know. For "out here", it is a scientifically accepted fact that the sun is "out there" 93 million miles away from earth. Yet:

> The rays of the sun are sun's unmediated expression, which is to say that are indivisible and not separate from the sun by one iota. This is analogous to how the waves of the ocean are not separate from the ocean, but are the unmediated manifestation of the ocean. This realization instantaneously helps us to change our perspective and understand that the sun is not outside of us, but rather as we are enveloped in its rays and a wash in its life-giving warmth we are inside of the sun. Not only do we find ourselves within the sun. This is to simultaneously realize that it makes just as much sense to think of the sun being inside us, which is an expression of our identity expanding to even larger degrees.
>
> – Levy 2019: 271-72

However, according to Pratyabhijñā (Recognition) school of Kashmir Śaivism of Indian philosophy, the "out there" (objectivities or external) and "out here" (subjectivity or internal) are explained very well in consciousness (awareness) of human being. This is stated below:

> Awareness serves to relate objectivity (external) and subjectivity

> (internal) in such way that the object ultimately comes to rest in the self-awareness of the subject. In reality, reflective awareness is always awareness of "I" (*ahaṁvimarśā*): it never object objectivises even when, in the form of the awareness of "this" (*idaṁvimarśā*), it reflects upon the object. The experience we have of things existing outside consciousness is due to lack of self-awareness. The awareness is never "out there"; it is registered and known within the subject. All forms of awareness come to rest in the subject. Just as every drop of water comes to rest in the ocean; so all acts and cognition (come to rest) in the great Lord of consciousness. – Dyczkowski 2006: 71
>
> This observation may be reassured by the statement that without consciousness, nothing in experienced, either "in here" or "out there". – Chopara and Kafatos on YouTube

Time and space are created as illusions. This is stated below:

i. The doctrine that time and space are illusions created in the mind not a mere interesting philosophical concept which has been evolved by intellectual analysis for the amusement of philosophers (Taimni 2005: 336).

ii. Bishop Berkeley, a philosopher, believed that all material objects and space and time are an illusion (Hawking 1988: 18).

The illusions seem to have taken place mainly because time and space are treated separately. Whereas the fact is that both time and space are one. Without time, space has no meaning. Similar is the case with space, which requires time for observing the events in human life. In this context, the following statements are relevant:

i. Space and its time are in like manner not two things but one, and there is no space without time nor time with space (Alexander 1927: 39).

ii. The error arises from separating time from space (ibid.: 234).

However, "time and space are one. One cannot be without other" (Hanh 2008: 201). Further, time and space have no independent existence because they are known by self-conscious human being. In fact, time and space inter-are. We cannot separate one from other. "Both are manifestations of consciousness" (Hanh 2008: 180). In other words, time and space both become the object of self-consciousness of human being. Consciousness is indeed all the heart of everything: time, space and the four great elements: earth, water, fire and air, are all displays of consciousness.

> All have the nature of inter-being: if we look deeply one, we find the other five. Looking into space we see time and other elements as well.
> – Ibid.: 181

However, N.C. Panda has mentioned that particles are conscious. At another place David Bohm, a well-known scientist, has also mentioned that even inanimate matter must have some kind of mental aspect. Unfortunately both are not correct. Particles cannot be conscious because they do not have mind and without mind nothing can be conscious. Same is the case with inanimate matter. It cannot have mental aspect, because it has no mind.

Bohm has also mentioned that the implicate order of quantum physics has implicate order. This comprehend both cosmos and consciousness as single unbroken totality of movement. This implicate order in a way to represent ourselves as the order present to the senses.

However, Bohm has also evolved the concept of "holomovement" with a view to capture dynamic phenomenon of which all forms of the material universe flow.

The aim of this approach is to study the order enfolded in this holomovement; not by dealing with the structure of objects, but rather with the structure of movement, thus taking into account both the unity and dynamic nature of the universe. According to Bohm, space and time emerge as forms flowing out of the holomovement; they too are enfloded in its order (Capra 1989: 353).

To understand the implicate order, Bohm thought that it was necessary to regard consciousness as an essential feature of the holomovement and to take it into account explicitly in his theory (Capra 1989: 353). However, according to Bohm, mind and matter are independent and are correlated to each other, but not causally connected (ibid.).

In the quantum field theory, the implicate order and the causal interpretation are quite simple. It is stated that

> instead of taking a particle as the fundamental reality, state with field. ... The field is continuous and by itself would tend to spread out from any source. However, because the super-quantum potential is non-linear and non-local, it is able under certain conditions, to provide a subtle kind of immediate connection between distant regions of the field. – Bohm and Peat 1987: 182

"In the causal interpretation of field theory, ... there are two implicate orders in a specified relationship" (ibid.: 182). The first implicate order is the field; itself and its movement. The second implicate order is explained as follows:

> The second implicate order under is then obtained by considering the super-quantum wave function. This is related to the whole field as the original quantum wave function is related to the particle. A more detailed treatment shows that the super-quantum wave function also moved in a kind of implicate order which is, however, for subtler and more complex than the first implicate order. This there comprises the second implicate order.
>
> – Ibid.: 182-83

According to Bohm and Peat, consciousness happens to partake much more of the implicate order than that of matter (ibid.: 185). Consciousness is captured by thought process which is definitely the implicate order. The word implicate means enfolded. It suggests that one thought enfolds other. However, the main approach adopted by Bohm and Peat (1987: 211-12) regarding consciousness is given below:

i. Consciousness has two aspects: (a) material, and (b) mental. The material aspect can be studied scientifically.

But the mental aspect would be rather difficult to capture by scientific studies. Therefore, one has to go beyond the usual approaches in which the mind and the matter are two separate but interacting streams.

ii. The root of the manifestation lies in the ultimate depths of the implicate and generative orders of the totality of matter, life and mind. In this context, it has been observed that "*even inanimate matter must have some kind of mental aspect*" (emphasis added by italics).

iii. There is no absolutely sharp "cut" or break between consciousness, life and matter whether animate or inanimate. Therefore, it has been concluded that as the consciousness approached to its origin of generative order, the mental aspect becomes more important, "While in the journey of 'downstream', the manifest physical side becomes more evident".

Bibliography

Acharya Narendradeva, 2001, *Baudha Dharma Darshan*, Delhi: Motilal Banarsidass.

Acharya, Sri Ananda, 1985, *Tattvajñānam or The Quest of Cosmic Consciousness*, Hoshiarpur: Vishveshvaranand Vedic Research Institute.

Adhvarindra, 2000, *Vedanta Paribhasa*, Calcutta: Advaita Ashram.

Agarwal, M.M., 1991, *Consciousness and Integrated Being*, New Delhi: National Publishing House.

Alexander, S., 1927, *Space, Time and Deity*, vol. II.

Alston, A.J. (tr.), 1997, *The Method of the Vedānta of Swami Satchidanandendra: A Critical Account of the Advaita Vedānta*, Delhi: Motilal Banarsidass.

Aung, S.Z., 1979, *Compendium of Philosophy*, London: The Pali Text Society.

Aurobindo, Sri, 2001, *The Life Divine*, Pondicherry: Sri Aurobindo Ashram.

———, 2002, *The Synthesis of Yoga*, Pondicherry: Sri Aurobindo Ashram.

Balasubramanian, R., 2004, "Advaita Vedānta on the Problem of Enworlded Subjectivity", in *Phenomenology and Indian Philosophy*, ed. D.P. Chattopadhyaya, L. Embree and J. Mohanty, New Delhi: Indian Council of Philosophical Research.

Balsekar, R.S., 1998, *Pointers from Nisargadatta Maharaj*, Bombay: Chetana.

Balslev, A.N., 1999, *A Study of Time in Indian Philosophy*, New Delhi: Munshiram Manoharlal.

Balsys, B., 2006, *Karma and the Rebirth of Consciousness*, New Delhi: Munshiram Manoharlal.

Barborka, G.A., 1998, *The Divine Plan*, Chennai: The Theosophical Publishing House.

Bart, W.H., 1995, *Philosophy of Knowledge*, vols I and II, ed. H.L. Mansel and John Veitch, Delhi: Ajay Book Service.

Besant, A., 2000, *Man and His Bodies*, Chennai: The Theosophical Publishing House.

Bhadra, M.M., 2004, *A Critical Survey of Phenomenology and Existentialism*, New Delhi: Indian Council of Philosophical Research.

Bhagavan Ramana Maharshi, 1999, *Absolute Consciousness,* tr. G.L.M. Martin, Bangalore: Raman Maharshi Centre for Learning.

———, 2002, *Self-Abidance: Sat-Darshanam,* tr. G. Kameshar, Bangalore: Ramana Maharshi Centre for Learning.

Bhatt, G., 1989, *The Basic Ways of Knowing*, Delhi: Motilal Banarsidass.

Bhattacharya, K., 1992, *Advaita-Siddhiḥ of Madhusūdana Sarasvatī,* New Delhi: Indian Council of Philosophical Research.

Bhattacharyya, K.C., 1983, *Studies in Philosophy*, ed. G. Bhattacharyya, Delhi: Motilal Banarsidass.

Bhattacharyya, S., 2004, "Phenomenology and Indian Philosophy", in *Phenomenology and Indian Philosophy*, New Delhi: Indian Council of Philosophical Research.

Bhaumik, M., 2005, *Code Name God: The Spritual Odyssey of a Man of Science*, Penguin Books.

Bhikkhu Bodhi (gen. ed.), 1999, *A Comprehensive Manual of Abhidhamma: The Abhidhammattha of Ācārya Anuruddha*, Kandy, Sri Lanka: Buddhist Publication Society.

Bohm, D., 2012, *Wholeness and the Implicate Order*, Routledge Classics, 1st Indian Repr., New Delhi: Routledge.

———, 2018, *On Dialogue*, New York: Routledge Classics, repr.

Bohm, D. and F.D. Peat, 1987, *Science, Order and Creativity*, New York: Bantam Books.

Boisvert, M., 1997, *The Five Aggregates*, Delhi: Sri Satguru Publications.

Brown, B.E., 1994, *The Buddha Nature: A Study of Thathagatagarbha and Ālaya-vijñāna*, Delhi: Motilal Banarsidass.

Capra, F., 1989, *The Tao of Physics*, London: Fontana Paperbacks.

Capra, F. and P.L. Luisi, 2014, *The Systems View of Life: A Unifying Vision*, Cambridge: Cambridge University Press.

Catalina, F.V., 1968, *A Study of the Self: Concept of the Sāṁkhya-Yoga Philosophy*, Delhi: Munshiram Manoharlal.

Chakrabarti, K.K., 2001, *Classical Indian Philosophy of Mind: The Nyāya Dualist Tradition*, Delhi: Motilal Banarsidass.

Chakraborty, N.B. (comp.), 2003, *A Dictionary of Advaita Vedānta*, Kolkata: The Ramakrishna Mission Institute of Culture.

Chang, G.C.C. (gen. ed.), 1983, *A Treasury of Mahāyāna Sūtras: Selection from the Mahāratnakūṭasūtra*, University Park and London: The Pennsylvania State University Press.

Chatterjee, A.K., 1999, *The Yogācāra Idealism*, Delhi: Motilal Banarsidass.

Chatterjea, T., S. Basu and A. Chatterjee (eds), 2014, *J.N. Mohanty Lectures on Kant's Pure Reason*, New Delhi: Munshiram Manoharlal.

Chatterjee, S. and D.M. Dutta, 1950, *An Introduction to Indian Philosophy*, Calcutta: University of Calcutta.

Chattopadhyay, N.K., 1979, *Indian Philosophy*, Calcutta: Sanskrit Pustak Bhandar.

Chaudhury, S., 1983, *Analytical Study of the Abhidharmakośa*, Calcutta: Firma KLM.

Christenson, W.J., 2011, "Does the Universe Have Cosmological Memory and Does This Imply Cosmic Consciousness?," *Journal of Cosmology*, 14.

Collins, S., 1982, *Selfless Persons: Imagery and Thought*, Cambridge, NY: Cambridge University Press.

Cross, S., 2014, *Schopenhauer's Encounter with Indian Thought*, New Delhi: Munshiram Mancharlal.

Datta, D.M., 1998, *The Six Ways of Knowing*, Calcutta: University of Calcutta.

Datt, N., 1978, *Mahāyāna Buddhism*, Delhi: Motilal Banarsidass.

de Silva, L.A., 1975, *The Problem of the Self in Buddhism and Christianity*, Colombo: The Study Centre for Religion and Society.

Devdas, N., 2008, *Cetanā and the Dynamics of Volition in Theravāda Buddhism*, Delhi: Motilal Banarsidass.

Dravid, N.S., 1995, *Atmatattvaviveka by Udayanācārya*, Simla: Indian Institute of Advanced Study.

Dyczkowski, M.S.G., 2006, *The Doctrine of Vibration: An Analysis of the Doctrines and Practice of Kashmir Shaivism*, Delhi: Motilal Banarsidass.

Ergardt, J., 1986, *Man and His Destiny*, Leiden: E.J. Brill.

Falkenburg, B., 2007, *Particle Metaphysics: A Critical Account of Subatomic Reality*, Berlin, Heidelberg: Springer-Verlag.

Ganguly, S. (tr)., 1992, *Treatise in Thirty Verses on Mere Consciousness*, Delhi: Motilal Banarsidass.

Garfield, J.L., 1995, *The Fundamental Wisdom of the Middle Way: Nāgārjuna's Mūlamadhyamakakārikā,* Oxford: Oxford University Press.

Glattfeldor, J.B., 2019, Information–Consciousness–Reality, London: Springer Open.

Godman, D. (ed.), 1992, *Be As You Are: The Teachings of Sri Ramana Maharshi,* New Delhi: Penguin Books.

Goswami, A., 1995, *The Self Aware Universe: How Consciousness Creates the Material World*, New York: Penguin.

Griffiths, P.J., 1999, *On Being Mindless,* Delhi: Sri Satguru Publications.

Grimes, J., 1992, *The Naiṣkarmyasiddhi of Sureśvara: A Monograph*, Delhi: Sri Satguru Publications.

Gupta, B., 2003, *Cit-consciousness*, New Delhi: Oxford University Press.

Haldar, A., 2001, *Some Psychological Aspects of Early Buddhist Philosophy Based on Abhidharmakoṣa of Vasubandhu*, Kolkata: The Asiatic Society.

Hanh, T., 2008, *Understanding Our Mind*, New Delhi: Harper Collins.

Hawking, S.W., 1988, *A Brief History of Time*, London: Bantam Press.

Hegel, G.W.F., 1998, *Phenomenology of Spirit*, Delhi: Motilal Banarsidass.

Hoffe, O., 2010, *Kant's Critique of Pure Reason: The Foundation of Modern Philosophy*, Dordrecht, Heidelberg, London, New York: Springer.

Hopkins, J., 2006, *Reflections on Reality*, Delhi: Motilal Banarsidass.

Hume, D., 1951, *A Treatise of Human Nature*, vol. I, London: J.M. Dent and Sons and New York: E.P. Dutton & Co.

Indich, W.M., 2000, *Consciousness in Advaita Vedānta*, Delhi: Motilal Banarsidass.

Jha, G. (tr.), 1986, *Tattvasaṅghraha of Shāntaraksita with Commentary of Kamalshila*, vol. II, Delhi: Motilal Banarsidass.

Joshi, M.M., 2006, "Life, Mind and Consciousness", in the Papers Read at a Seminar Published in *Life, Mind and Consciousness*, Kolkata: The Ramakrishna Mission Institute of Culture.

Kalupahana, D.J., 1992a, *The Principles of Buddhist Psychology*, Delhi: Sri Satguru Publications.

———, 1992b, *Mūlamadhyamakakārikā of Nāgārjuna*, Delhi: Motilal Banarsidass.

Kameshwar, G. (tr.), 2007, *Self-Abidance Sat-Darśanam*, Bangalore: Ramana Maharishi Centre for Learning.

Kant, I., 1950, *The Critique of Pure Reason*, tr. J.M.D. Meiklejohn, London: Dent and Sons.

Kapani, L., 2013, *The Philosophical Concept of Saṁskāras*, Delhi: Motilal Banarsidass.

Kher, C.V., 1992, *Buddhism as Presented by the Brahmanical Systems*, Delhi: Sri Satguru Publications.

Kochumuttom, T.A., 1999, *A Buddhist Doctrine of Experience*, Delhi: Motilal Banarsidass.

Kothari, D.S., 2002, "Atom and Self", Meghnad Saha Medal Lecture 1978 delivered at INSA, New Delhi, 5 October 1979. This is published in F. Ahmad (ed.), *Collection of Lectures Delivered by D.S. Kothari*, New Delhi: New Age International.

Krishnamurti, J., 1992/2007, *Choiceless Awareness*, Ojai, CA: Krishnamurti Foundation of America.

———, 1997, *Reflections on the Self*, ed. Raymond Martin, Chicago: Open Court.

Laksmithathachar, M.A., 2003, "Study of Consciousness from the Point of View of Viśiṣṭādvaita Philosophy", in *Understanding Consciousness: Recent Advances*, ed. Swami Sarvabhutananda, Kolkata: Ramakrishna Mission Institute of Culture.

Lanza, R. and B. Berman, 2009, *Biocentrism: How Life and Consciousness Are the Keys to Understanding the True Nature of the Universe*, Dallas, TX: Benbella Books.

Larson, G.J., 2003, "The Anthropic Principle: Life Cosmos and Consciousness", in *Philosophy and Science: An Exploratory Approach to Consciousness*, Paper read at the Seminar held at the Ramakrishna Mission Institute of Culture, Kolkata, 8 and 9 February 2002, Kolkata: Ramakrishna Mission Institute of Culture.

———, 2009, "The Notion of 'Consciousness' as Witness in Indian Philosophy and Modern Science", in *Life, Mind and Consciousness*, papers read at a seminar held at Ramakrishna Mission Institute of Culture, Kolkata on 16-18 January 2014, ed. Swami Prabhananda, Kolkata: Ramakrishna Mission Institute of Culture.

Larson, G.J. and R.S. Bhattacharya, 1987, *Encyclopedia of Indian Philosophy*, vol. IV: *Saṁkhyā*, Delhi: Motilal Banarsidass.

Levy, J., 2004, *The Nature of Man According to the Vedānta*, Boulder, CO: Sentient Publications.

Levy, P., 2019, *A Physics of Possibilities: Explore of the World of Quantum Spirituality*, Mumbai: Jaico Publishing House.

Limaye, S.V. (tr.), 2000, *Mahāyānasūtrālaṁkāra by Asaṅga*, Delhi: Sri Satguru Publications.

Macy, J., 1991, *Mutual Causality in Buddhism and General Systems Theory: The Dharma of Natural Systems*, Albany, NY: SUNY Press.

Manju, 1986, अद्वैतवाद और शून्यवाद, Delhi: Eastern Book Linkers.

Masih, Y., 2002, *A Critical History of Western Philosophy*, Delhi: Motilal Banarsidass.

Matilal, B.K., 1986, *Perception: An Essay on Classical Indian Theories of Knowledge*, Oxford: Clarendon Press.

———, 1997, *Logic, Language and Reality*, Delhi: Motilal Banarsidass.

Maturana, H.R. and F.J. Varela, 1979, *Autopoiesis and Cognition*, Dordrecht: D. Reidel.

Mcdermott, J.P., 1999, "Karma and Rebirth in Early Buddhism", in *Karma and Rebirth in Classical Indian Traditions*, ed. W.D. Oflaherty, Delhi: Motilal Banarsidass.

McCormick, A. (illustrations by), 2001, *The Mystery of Creation*, Bombay: Central Chinmaya Mission Trust.

Medhidhammaporn, P., 1995, *Sartre's Existentialism and Early Buddhism*, Bangkok: Buddhadhamma Foundation.

Meiklejohn, J.M.D. (tr.), 2010-13, *The Critique of Pure Reason by Immanuel Kant*, An Electronic Classics Series Publication, University Park, PA: The Pennsylvania State University.

Menon, M.G.K., 2004, "What We Know from Science about the Origin and Evolution of Life: Its Relevance to the Issues of Mind and Consciousness", in *Life, Mind and Consciousness*, papers read at an Internal Seminar held at the Ramakrishna Mission Institute of Culture, Kolkata, during 16-18 January 2004, ed. Swami Prabhananda.

Merleau-Ponty, M., 2005, *Phenomenology of Perception*, New York: Routledge.

Miller, A.V. (tr.), 1998, *Phenomenology of Spirit of Hegel G.W.F.*, Delhi: Motilal Banarsidass.

Misra, V.N., 2014, *Science of Consciousness: A Synthesis of Vedānta and Buddhism*, New Delhi: Munshiram Manoharlal.

Mittal, K.K. (ed.), 1990, *Perspectives on Karma and Rebirth*, Delhi: University of Delhi.

Mohanty, J.N., 1995, "Some Aspects of Indian Thinking on Being", in *The Question of Being: East-West Perspective*, ed. Sprung Mervyn, Delhi: Sri Satguru Publications.

Mohanty, J.N. and S.P. Banerjee, 1978, *Self, Knowledge and Freedom*, Calcutta: The World Press.

Moitra, S., 1988, "Alternative Standpoints at the Foundation and Culmination of Kalidas Bhattacharyya's Philosophy", in *Freedom, Transcendence and Identity*, ed. P.K. Sengupta, New Delhi: Indian Council of Philosophical Research, This is based on Kalidas Bhattacharyya, 1953, *Alternative Standpoints in Philosophy*, Calcutta: Dasgupta & Co.

Mookerjee, S., 1993, *The Buddhist Philosophy of Universal Flux*, Delhi: Motilal Banarsidass.

Mukerji, A.C., 1938, *The Nature of Self*, Allahabad: The Indian Press.

———, 1957, *Self, Thought and Reality*, Allahabad: The Juvenile Press.

Mukhopadhyaya, M.M.G., 2004, "The Intrinsic Nature of Consciousness and Its Different Manifestations as Envisaged in Different Systems of Indian Philosophy", in *Life, Mind and Consciousness*, ed. Swami Prabhananda, Kolkata: Ramakrishna Mission Institute of Culture.

Murti, T.R.V., 2003, *The Central Philosophy of Buddhism: A Study of Mādhyamika System*, New Delhi: Munishiram Manoharlal.

Narlikar, J., 1978, *The Structure of the Universe*, London/Oxford: Oxford University Press.

Organ, T.W., 1988, *The Self and Its Worlds: East and West*, Selingrove:

Susquehanna University Press; London and Toronto: Associated University Press.

Panda, N.C., 2008, *Māyā in Physics*, Delhi: Motilal Banarsidass.

Pandit, M.L., 1993, *Being as Becoming: Studies in Early Buddhism*, New Delhi: Intercultural Publications.

———, 2008, *The Buddhist View of Knowledge and Reality*, New Delhi: Munshiram Manoharlal.

Piatigorsky, A., 1984, *The Buddhist Philosophy of Thought*, London: Curson Press.

Potter, K.H., 1998, *Encyclopedia of Indian Philosophy*, vol. III: *Advaita Vedānta up to Śaṅkara and His Pupils*, Delhi: Motilal Banarsidass.

Powell, A.E., 2005, *The Causal Body and the Ego*, Adyar (Chennai): The Theosophical Publishing House.

Prasad, H.S., 1990, "The Buddhist Doctrine of Karma", in *Perspectives on Karma and Rebirth*, ed. K.K. Mittal, Delhi: University of Delhi.

Prasad, Swami Muni Narayana, 1994, *The Taittirīya Upaniṣad*, New Delhi: D.K. Printworld.

———, 1998, *Muṇḍaka Upaniṣad*, New Delhi: D.K. Printworld.

———, 1999, *Praśna Upaniṣad*, New Delhi: D.K. Printworld.

———, 2004, *Kaṭha Upaniṣad*, New Delhi: D.K. Printworld.

———, 2006a, *Chāndogya Upaniṣad*, New Delhi: D.K. Printworld.

———, 2006b, *Karma and Reincarnation*, New Delhi: D.K. Printworld.

———, 2009, *Īśavāsya and Māṇḍūkya Upaniṣads*, New Delhi: D.K. Printworld.

Pruden, L.M. (tr.), 1991, *Abhidharmakośabhāṣyam*, vol. I by Louis La Vallée Poussin, Berkeley, CA: Asian Humanities Press.

Radhakrishnan, S., 2002, *Indian Philosophy*, vol. II, New Delhi: Oxford University Press.

———, 2005, *The Dhammapada*, New Delhi: Oxford University Press.

———, 2009, *The Principal Upaniṣads*, New Delhi: Harper Collins.

Rajagopal, L.V., 1993, *A Critique of Vedānta*, New Delhi: Munshiram Manoharlal.

Ram, K., 1995, *Integral Non-Dualism*, Delhi: Motilal Banarsidass.

Ranasinghe, C.P., 1957, *The Buddha's Explanation of the Universe*, Colombo: Lanka Bauddha Mandalaya Fund.

Rangaswami, S., 2012, *The Roots of Vedanta*, New Delhi: Penguin Books.

Reat, N.R., 1990, *Origins of Indian Psychology*, Berkeley, CA: Asian Humanities Press.

Rene, G., 1981, *Man and His Becoming According to Vedānta*, New Delhi: Oriental Books Reprint Corporation.

Robert, T.A.F. (tr.), 2001, *The Tibetan Book of the Dead*, New Delhi: Harper Collins.

Roy, K., 2013, *Subjectivity in Science: Interpretations of the Cartesian Project*, Kolkata: Ramakrishna Mission Institute of Culture.

Sadhu, Santinatha, 1938, *The Critical Examination of the Philosophy and Religion*, vol. II, Amalner: Pratap Seth.

Safaya, R., 1976, *Indian Psychology*, New Delhi: Munshiram Manoharlal.

Saksena, S.K., 1971, *Nature of Consciousness in Indian Philosophy*, Delhi: Motilal Banarsidass.

Sarasvati, Madhusudana, 2007, *Bhagavadgītā with the Annotation Gūḍhārtha Dīpikā*, tr. Swami Gambhirananda, Kolkata: Advaita Ashrama.

Sarbadhikari, A., 1991, *Mill's Self Regarding Acts: An Analysis*, Simla: Indian Institute of Advanced Study, in association with Munshiram Manoharlal, New Delhi.

Sartre, J.-P., 1984, *Being and Nothingness*, tr. Hazel E. Barnes, New York: Washington Square Press.

Sastri, S.S.S. and C.K. Raja (tr.), 1992, *Bhāmatī of Vācaspati*, Madras: The Adyar Library and Research Centre.

Seal, B., 1985, *The Positive Sciences of the Ancient Hindus*, Delhi: Motilal Banarsidass.

Searle, J.R., 2004, *Mind: A Brief Introduction*, New York: Oxford University Press.

Sharma, C.D., 2003, *A Critical Survey of Indian Philosophy*, Delhi: Motilal Banarsidass.

Shrivastava, S.N.L., 1968, *Śaṅkara and Bradley: A Comparative and Critical Study*, Delhi: Motilal Banarsidass.

Sinari, R.K., 2007, *The Paradox of Being Human*, New Delhi: Indian Council of Philosophical Research.

Singh, S.P., 2004, *Vedic Vision of Consciousness and Reality*, New Delhi: PHISPC-Centre for Studies in Civilizations.

Sinha, J., 1971, *A History of Indian Philosophy*, vol. III, Calcutta: Sinha Publishing House and Motilal Banarsidass, Delhi.

Sinha, J.N., 1958, *Indian Psychology: Cognition*, vol. I, Calcutta: Sinha Publishing House.

———, 1999, *Indian Realism*, Delhi: Motilal Banarsidass.

———, 2006, *Indian Philosophy*, vol. II, repr., Delhi: Motilal Banarsidass.

Sinha, N.L., 2013, *The Sāṁkhya Philosophy*, New Delhi: Munshiram Manoharlal.

Sogen, Y., 2002, *Systems of Buddhist Thought*, New Delhi: Cosmo Publications.

Sparham, G. in collaboration with Shotara (tr.), 1993, *Ocean of Eloquence: Tsongakhapa's Commentary on Yogācāra Doctrine of Mind*, New York: SUNY Press.

Śrī Śaṅkarācārya, 2008, *Śrīmad Bhagavadgītā Bhāṣya*, Madras: Sri Ramakrishna Math.

Sri Sri Paramahansa Yogananda, 2007, *The Bhagavad Gītā*, vol. I, Kolkata: Yogoda Satsanga Society of India.

Srinivasan, G., 1994, *Insights into Inward Consciousness*, New Delhi: Indian Council of Philosophical Research.

Stcherbatsky, T. (tr.), 1978, *Madhyānta-Vibhaṅga*, New Delhi: Oriental Books Reprint Corporation.

———, 1983, *The Central Conception of Buddhism*, Delhi: Motilal Banarsidass.

———, 1996, *Buddhist Logic*, vol. I, New Delhi: Munshiram Manoharlal.

———, 2003, *The Conception of Buddhist Nirvāṇa*, Delhi: Motilal Banarsidass.

Suzuki, D.T., 1999, *Studies in the Laṅkāvatārasūtra*, Delhi: Motilal Banarsidass.

———, 2000, *Outlines of Mahāyāna Buddhism*, New Delhi: Munshiram Manoharlal.

Swami Atmapriyananda, 2006, "Bhavamukha: Sri Ramakrishna's Unique Contribution to the Science of Consciousness", in *Consciousness: A Deeper Scientific Search*, the paper read in a seminar held at the Ramakrishna Mission Institute of Culture, Kolkata, Kolkata: Ramakrishna Mission Institute of Culture.

Swami Bhajananda, 2009, "Knowledge and Consciousness: An Integral Approach", in *Understanding Consciousness: Recent Advances*, papers read at a seminar held at the Ramakrishna Institute of Culture, Kolkata, 18-20 January 2008, Kolkata: Ramakrishna Mission Institute of Culture.

Swami Gambhirananda (tr.), 2000, *Brahmasūtra Bhāṣya of Śrī Śaṅkarācārya*, Kolkata: Advaita Ashrama.

——— (tr.), 2003, *Chāndogya Upaniṣad*, Calcutta: Advaita Ashrama.

——— (tr.), 2004, *Taittirīya Upaniṣad with Commentary of Śaṅkarācārya*, Kolkata: Advaita Ashrama.

——— (tr.), 2007, *Bhagavad Gītā of Madhusudana Sarasvati*, Kolkata: Advaita Ashrama.

Swami Jagadananda (tr.), 2000, *Upadeśa Sāhasrī of Śrī Śaṅkarācārya*, Madras: Sri Ramakrishna Math.

Swami Jitātmānanda, 1993, *Holistic Science and Vedānta*, based on the book *Quantum Questions* by K. Wilber, Shambhala Publications, New York, 1984, Bombay: Bhartiya Vidya Bhawan.

Swami Madhavananda (tr.), 1997, *The Bṛhadāraṇyaka Upaniṣad with Commentary of Śaṅkarācārya*, Calcutta: Advaita Ashrama.

——— (tr.), 2000, *Vedānta-Paribhāṣā of Dharmarāja Adhvarīndra*, Calcutta: Advaita Ashrama.

Swami Mukhyananda, 2006, *Sri Shankaracharya: Life and Philosophy: An Elucidative and Reconciliatory Interpretation*, Kolkata: Advaita Ashrama.

Swami Nikhilananda (tr.), 2000, *The Māṇḍūkya Upaniṣad with Gauḍapāda's Kārikā and Śaṅkara's Commentary*, Calcutta: Advaita Ashrama.

——— (tr.), 2008, *Self Knowledge of Śrī Śaṅkarācārya*, Chennai: Sri Ramakrishna Advaita Ashrama.

Swami Satprakashananda (tr.), 1974, *The Goal and the Way*, Madras (now Chennai): Sri Ramakrishna Math.

———, 2001a, *Methods of Knowledge*, Kolkata: Advaita Ashrama.

———, 2001b, *Mind According to Vedānta*, Madras: Sri Ramakrishna Math.

———, 2004, *The Universe God and God-Realization from the Viewpoint of Vedānta*, Chennai: Sri Ramakrishna Math.

Swami Swahananda (tr.), 2001, *Pañcadaśī of Śrī Vidyāraṇya Swāmī*, Chennai: Sri Ramakrishna Math.

Swami Tattwananda (tr.), 2002, *The Quintessence of Vedānta of Śrī Śaṅkarācārya*, Kalady, Ernakulam: Sri Ramakrishna Ashrama.

Swami Turiyananda (tr.), 2007, *Vivekacūḍāmaṇi of Śrī Śaṅkarācārya*, Chennai: Sri Ramakrishna Math.

Swami Virupakshananda (tr.), 2003, *Sāṁkhyakārikā of Īśvarakṛṣṇa*, Chennai: Sri Ramakrishna Math.

Swami Yogeshwaranand Saraswati, 1987, *Science of Soul*, Rishikesh: Yoga Niketan Trust.

Swami Yogindrananda, 2005, *Pramāṇavārttikam of Dharmakīrti*, vol. II, Varanasi: Chowkhamba Vidyabhawan.

Taimni, I.K., 1987a, *Glimpses into the Psychology of Yoga*, Madras: The Theosophical Publishing House.

———, 1987b, *Science and Occultism*, Madras: The Theosophical Publishing House.

———, 1998, *The Secret of Self Realization*, Chennai: The Theosophical Publishing House.

———, 1999, *The Science of Yoga*, Chennai: The Theosophical Publishing House.

———, 2005, *Man, God and the Universe*, Chennai: The Theosophical Publishing House.

Thanh, T.M., 2008, *The Mind in Early Buddhism*, New Delhi: Munshiram Manoharlal.

Thibaut, G. (tr.), 1994, *The Vivaraṇaprameya-Saṅgraha of Vidyāraṇya*, Delhi: Sri Satguru Publications.

Thomas, V.C., 2004, "Husserlian Foundations of Sartre's Treatment of Time Consciousness", in *Phenomenology and Indian Philosophy*, ed. D.P. Chattopadhyaya, L. Embree and J. Mohanty, New Delhi: Indian Council of Philosophical Research.

Tilak, B.G., 2000, *Srimad Bhagavad-Gita Rashaya*, Poona: Tilak Brothers.

Timalsina, S., 2006, *Seeing and Appearance*, Aachen, Germany: Shaker Verlag.

Tiwary, M. (ed.), 1988, *Namarupa-Paricchedo*, Delhi: Uttaranchal Cooperative Group Housing Society.

Tola, F. and C. Dragonetti, 2004, *Being as Consciousness*, Delhi: Motilal Banarsidass.

Upadhyaya, B.S., 2006, *Bauddha Philosophy and Other Indian Philosophy*, vol. I, Delhi: Motilal Banarsidass.

Upadhyaya, K.N., 1983, *Early Buddhism and the Bhagavadgītā*, Delhi: Motilal Banarsidass.

Waldron, W.S., 2003, *The Buddhist Unconscious: The Ālaya-vijñāna in the Context of Indian Buddhist Thought*, London and New York: Routledge–Curzon.

Warren, H.C., 2002, *Buddhism in Translations*, Delhi: Motilal Banarsidass.

Wilber, K., 2002, *The Spectrum of Consciousness*, Delhi: Motilal Banarsidass.

Williamson, R.K., 1984, *Introduction to Hegel's Philosophy of Religion*, Albany, NY: State University of New York Press.

Woodroffe, J., 2001, *The World as Power*, repr., Madras: Ganesh and Company.

Index